GHOST TOWNS OF MICHIGAN
VOLUME II

Larry Wakefield

WITHDRAWN

Holt, Michigan

Other titles by Larry Wakefield:

All Our Yesterdays, A Narrative history of Traverse City and the Region

The Mystery of the Missing Nun

Historic Traverse City Houses
(with Lucille Wakefield)

Sail & Rail, A History of Transportation in the Grand Traverse Region
(with Lucille Wakefield)

National Cherry Festival, An Illustrated History

Elmwood Township, An Illustrated History

Queen City of the North, An Illustrated History of Traverse City

Butcher's Dozen, 13 Famous Michigan Murders

Traverse City Postcard History

Leelanau County Postcard History

Ghost Towns of Michigan (Volume I)

Garfield Township, An Illustrated History

Once again, for Lucille

TABLE OF CONTENTS

Bingham and the *Leelanau*	1
Norwood and the Indian Chert Mine	6
Printer, Griner, and Nessen City	11
Sparr Has Only One Mall	17
Waters and the Glass Bottle Fence	22
Hallock Had a Gold Mine	27
Lonesome Pere Cheney	32
Haring and the Shay Locomotive	37
Berryville Perished in a Fire	43
Crawfords Quarry Got Swallowed Up	47
The Metz Tragedy	52
Alcona and the Log Rafts	59
Potts-McKinley and Mr. Davis	64
The "Lost" Gold Mine of Harrisville	70
Pearl Harbor Made Mikado Mad	75
The Lost City of Damon	80
Fouch: Where Boats and Railroad Met	84
Manistee County's "Mystery House"	90
Meredith Was a Wicked Town	94
Selkirk: A River Runs Through It	101
Herron Had a Uranium Mine	107
Alba Had No Water	112
Meredith Revisited	120
Colonville and Train Robber, John Smalley	127
Leer and the Sinkholes	132
Antrim City Died Aborning	140
Levi Lupton Was a Rascal But He Built a Town	145
Comins: End of the Line	153
Essex Disappeared	160
Shelldrake and Irishman Con Culhane	165

Whitefish Point: Cranberries,
    Whitefish, Shipwrecks 172
Thompsonville: The Biggest Little
    Town in Michigan 178
Podunk's Still There 185
Mayfield Had Its Ups and Downs 190
Park Lake and Ghost Creek 195
Crofton Was a Hard Luck Town 200
Mitchell Had a Grist Mill 205
South Boardman Was Crippled By Fire 210
Pennock and the Railroad War 216
Williamsburg Had a Gas Blowout 221
The Indians Called It Wekwagamaw 227
Stittsville Had Hopes 231
Springvale Went from Rags to Riches 237
Falmouth and the Ancient Indian Village 244
Stover on the River 250
Growing up at Fiborn Quarry 256
Harrietta: Still a Good Place to Live 261

> The pictures in this book are attributed where known. The Publisher apologizes for any specific pictures we may have used without proper permission.

ACKNOWLEDGMENTS

For historic material and/or photographs I am indebted to the following people: Julius Petertyl, Steve Harold, and Ken Shugart of Traverse City; Phebe Cotton and Rena Bellinger, Kalkaska; Joe Murphy, Grayling; Bonnie Griner, Interlochen; Ira House and Phyllis Boughner, Sparr; Marvin and Rhoda Kelso, Hallock; Mrs. Earl Perrin, Fouch; Jim Annis, Alba; Bill Beuche, Suttons Bay; Howard Yount, Lake City; Terry Wooten, Kewadin; Bob Boven, Falmouth; Linda Record, Ellsworth; Max Sneary, Marion; Charlie Conn, Gaylord; Linda Christopherson, Leer, Julie Wilber, Empire, and Nelson Yoder, Comins.

My thanks also to the following institutions: Traverse Area District Library, Grand Traverse Pioneer & Historical Society, Northwestern Michigan College's Mark and Helen Osterlin Library, Bayliss Public Library (Sault Ste. Marie), Rose City Public Library, Grayling Public Library, Missaukee County Public Library (Lake City), Harrison Public Library, and Alpena Public Library.

All of these stories appeared originally in the Summer Magazine of the *Traverse City Record Eagle*, and I am grateful to the editors for permission to publish them here.

I also want to thank Dan Nielsen of the *Record Eagle* for his maps which accompany each story and add much to its presentation.

Copyright © 1995 by Larry Wakefield

All rights reserved. No part of this book may be used or reproduced in any manner without prior written permission of the publisher, except in the case of brief quotations embodied in critical reviews and articles.

Printed in the United States of America
95 96 97 98 99   1 2 3 4 5 6 7

ISBN: 1-882376-19-6

1
Bingham and the *Leelanau*

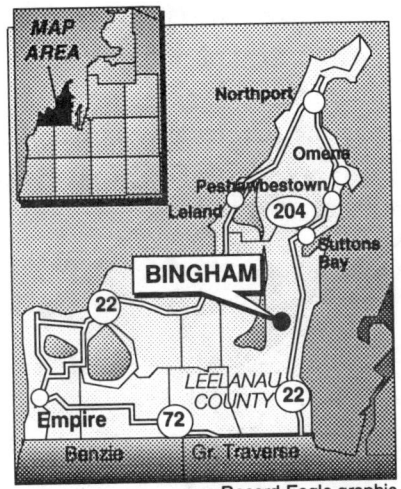
Record-Eagle graphic

Bingham was one of the many northern Michigan villages that owed their existence to a sawmill. The little farm community, scattered along the Northport-Newaygo State Road north of Traverse City, was awarded a post office in 1878; William Core was its first postmaster. But the town didn't really get started until 1881, when Boone and Johnson built a sawmill for S. C. Darrow on the east shore of Lake Leelanau, then called Carp

Lake. The pioneer Boones were direct descendants of Stephen Boone, brother of the famous Daniel.

The steam-powered mill cut an average of 12,000 board feet of hardwood lumber per day—this wasn't pine country and never had been. Darrow built a plank road along what is now Bingham Road and hauled his dressed lumber three miles over the hills to his dock on Grand Traverse Bay, whence it was shipped by schooner to Chicago. It was said that the steady stream of horses and wagons rattled the glasses and teacups in the farm family homes along the way.

Darrow lost the mill (and his shirt) to the Hannah Lay interests after shipping a load of mildewed lumber to Chicago. He not only didn't get paid for the lumber but he had to pay the freight. Down but not out, he moved to Traverse City, borrowed $3,200 from

John Larken and his lumberjacks and millworkers; Larkin at center in white shirt and vest. Courtesy of Ken Shugart.

the Greilick brothers and opened a grocery store which remained in the family for four generations. The building, much remodeled, still stands at 817 Bay Street, now the home of a window-covering store.

John Larkin, a mountain of a man with shoulders just a few inches narrower than a Mack truck, bought the mill on credit from Perry Hannah. Larkin didn't have a dime, but he had lots of lumbering experience and the mill prospered in his hands—attesting to Hannah's excellent judgement of character. The mill was later sold to Meinrod "Mike" Oberlin and still later to the Boughey family of the Traverse City Lumber Company.

Meanwhile, Bingham had grown to a town of more than thirty houses, a saloon and dance hall, and a big general store. There were at least three boarding houses for the mill workers. One was operated by Zimri Hinshaw, who also had a blacksmith shop. Logs were rafted to the mill by a steam tug on Carp Lake. Oliver Shugart and the Hockstad boys worked on the tug, often rafting logs through the OxBow Loop, as the tricky channel between the lakes at Provemont was called.

Beginning around 1894, Bingham Landing became an important stop for the steamer *Tiger*, which made two round trips daily between Leland and Fouch, where it met the newly arrived Manistee & Northeastern Railroad. Bingham people could catch the morning train at Fouch, spend seven hours in Traverse City, then ride the *Tiger* home that evening.

The Bingham school was built around 1896. Now completely restored, it serves as the Bingham Township Hall. Courtesy of Ken Shugart.

The Bingham store has long since disappeared.

In 1901, the steamer *Leelanau* entered competition with the *Tiger*. She was designed by Louis Hockstad of Bingham and built of heavy tamarack planking by Louis Mosier and his two sons. The intense rivalry between the two boats started a price war which reduced the round-trip fare from Leland to Fouch from $1.50 to $1.00, and then to 75 cents.

The *Leelanau* finally drove *Tiger* off the lake, but on August 16, 1908, she met with catastrophe. Just off Bingham Landing her vertical boiler blew up with a terrific roar. The blast threw passenger Isabelle LaBonte overboard; her body was found five days later. Ironically, John Hartung, former captain of the *Tiger*, was at the wheel when the explosion occurred. He was severely scalded by steam and boiling water and died a few days later.

The arrival of the Traverse City Leelanau & Manistique Railroad in 1902 gave the town a boost, but the timber was running out and the mill closed down in 1909. The big sawmill engine was crated up and shipped to a mill at Batchawana Bay on Lake Superior.

That, for all practical purposes, was the end of the town, too, though it lingered on, as ghosts are apt to do, for a few more years. The post office closed down in 1908.

Among other early family names are Donner, Heimforth, Hulbert, Dalzell, Porter, Weigand, and Eblacher. Many of them are still on the local mailboxes.

2
Norwood and the Indian Chert Mine

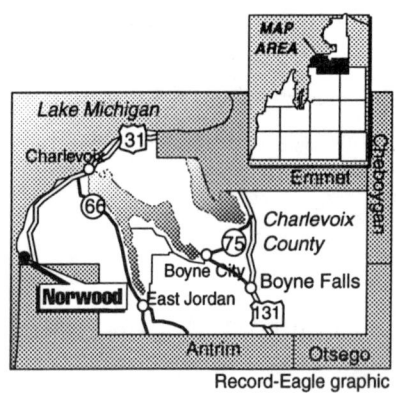

Record-Eagle graphic

Norwood was an important place to Michigan Indians long before it was called Norwood. The town lies on a bluff overlooking Lake Michigan eight miles south of Charlevoix at the mouth of Grand Traverse Bay. It has the same latitude as the tip of Leelanau County peninsula and was therefore the logical place where, for hundreds or perhaps thousands of years, the Indians made the "great crossing": The early French trappers and traders called it "le grande traverse." By paying close attention to the weather—a matter of instinct among Indians—they could make the seven-mile shortcut across the open water in their birch bark canoes without getting into trouble. There was an Indian village at Norwood.

The town itself got started in 1867, when Orvis Wood, Lucius Pearl, and Orin Adams built a dock and a sawmill there and began to cut the extensive hardwood timber in the area. They hired William Harris to run their sawmill boarding house. Legend has it that he came down from Charlevoix with his wife and two daughters in a rowboat, but that can't be quite right since one of the two daughters, Bertha, was the first white child to be born in Norwood.

In 1868 Harris built the first hotel in Norwood and became its first postmaster. The town took its name from its location in the north woods, or maybe

The Norwood school, built in 1890.

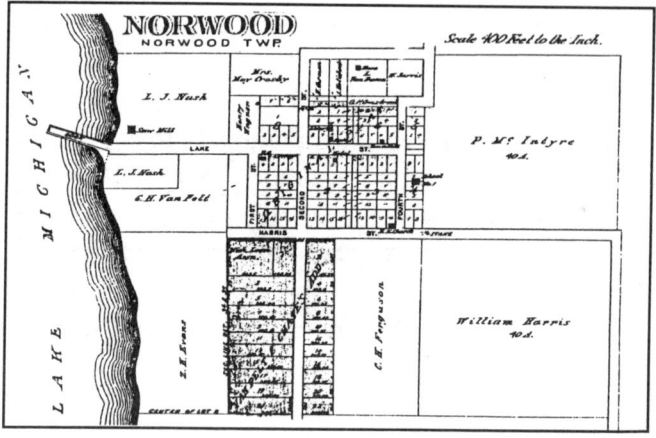

Plat map of Norwood.

from lumberman Wood. Harris also bought land in the area and became one of its most successful farmers. He was Marion Township's first supervisor when it was organized in 1867, and served at least nine terms as Norwood Township's supervisor after it was set off from Marion in 1869. Marion Township was named for Harris' wife.

Norwood thrived as long as the timber held out. During its heyday it had several sawmills, a big company store, blacksmith shop, shoe stores and several other businesses. In 1890 its population numbered around 400.

The first school was started in 1867 with Jasper Adams as its first teacher. The present building, owned by the United Methodist church, was built in 1890; it now serves as the community meeting place. The church itself was built in 1884.

The big Norwood sawmill. Courtesy of Charlevoix Historical Society.

Countless thousands of board feet of hardwood lumber passed over Norwood's big dock to be loaded into schooners and steamers for sale in Chicago and Milwaukee. Much of it went to rebuild the city of Chicago after the disastrous fire of 1871. Later, the town continued to be an important port of call for Bay steamers such as *Columbia*, *Crescent* and *Chequamegon*, based in Traverse City.

This odd-looking building was a windmill to supply water to Norwood residents. It also served as a bandstand. Courtesy of Charlevoix Historical Society.

But the big mill burned down in 1890 and Norwood lost its post office in 1913. In 1891, the Pere Marquette railroad missed Norwood by almost six miles. It suffered the crowning blow when US-31 was rerouted one-and-one-half miles to the east.

Norwood was an important place to the Indians for another reason. It was their source of chert, the stone from which they made arrowheads, knives and spear points. Chert, or hornstone, is an impure form of flint found in a variety of colors: white, yellow, gray and brown. Some of the prettiest stones are banded with translucent layers of white and gray. Like flint, it fractures conchoidally (shell-shaped), leaving razor-sharp edges. The Indian "chert mine" is a two-mile stretch of beach where the stone is found in great abundance.

The Indians are gone now, and the lumberjacks, and most of the people who once called Norwood home. But Norwood is still a lovely, sleepy little village with well-kept, traditionally-white houses (some of them more than a century old and restored to their original beauty), shade trees and immaculate green lawns. The natives and summer people do their shopping at Charlevoix but most of the time are quite content to enjoy pastoral peace and quiet and let the rest of the world go by.

3
Print, Griner and Nessen City

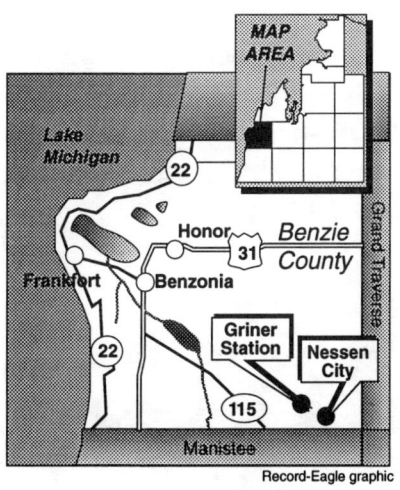
Record-Eagle graphic

Print and Griner Station were two names for the same backwoods place —one for the post office and the other for the stagecoach stop. Nessen City, a short distance away, came later.

Around 1875, John Griner built a traveller's inn in Section 26 of Colfax Township in Benzie County and established an east-west stagecoach line. Known as "Halfway House" because it lay half way between

The Nessen school was originally a two-story building; the upper story was removed to reduce expenses during the Depression. Courtesy of Bonnie Griner.

Benzonia and Traverse City, Griner Station was the logical place to rest and water the horses after climbing three big hills to the west, and to provide the passengers with a drink, a meal, a bed (or all three), depending on the time of day or night.

The Mix residence is one of the older homes at Nessen City.

Free-standing chimney of a burned-out house at Griner Station.

The old stagecoach trail east of Griner Station.

In 1879, Print (the name's origin is obscure) was awarded a post office with John Griner as postmaster. At the peak of its short life, Griner Station also had a store, a dance hall, and a school. In addition to the Griners, other pioneer families in the area were the Millirons and the Dingers; all came from Pennsylvania.

In 1889, the Manistee & Northeastern Railroad came through a mile away, and the village abruptly ceased to exist. The railroad killed the stagecoach and, like the Deacon's Masterpiece, Print-Griner Station came to its end "all at once, and nothing first—just as bubbles do when they burst."

That same year, Manistee lumberman John O. Nessen and his wife Edith platted the town of Nessen City on the railroad a mile-and-a-half southwest of Griner Station, and built a big sawmill on Peppermint Creek and a company store. Nessen, a native Swede, was one of the last of Michigan's fabled lumber barons—a short generation younger than such men as Perry Hannah, Louis Sands, R. G. Peters and Ed Buckley.

The town was "square with the world" and the railroad ran through it diagonally from southwest to northeast. Off to a good start, it soon began to fill with millworkers and their families. Businesses followed: another general store, built by George Bunting two blocks north of the Nessen store on Colfax Street; Hotel Northern, a 29-room hostelry with a saloon on the first floor and a big livery stable; another hotel, known as Mrs. McGrant's Boarding House, on Eglin Street. According to legend, at least seven saloons did business in town over the years.

The town prospered even after the big timber was cut. A hame factory took advantage of the abundance of rock elm in the area; the hames (a harness part) were roughed and cured at the factory, then shipped to Cincinnati to be finished with metal parts. Nearby cedar swamps kept several shingle mills in operation for many years. The town had a Catholic church and a two-story schoolhouse.

Unlike Griner Station, Nessen City's demise was slow: it just sort of withered away. Fires in 1897, 1903, and 1908 took their toll of the houses and buildings, the railroad was taken up in the 1930s and the town lost its post office soon after. Now its few residents are mainly people who work in nearby communities.

Train wreck on the M & NE at Nessen City. Courtesy of Michigan State University Archives & Historical Collection.

Griner Station, of course, is completely gone, but it's a nostalgic kind of place. Ruined foundations, a lone free-standing house chimney, and huge gnarled maples all combine to give the spine a tingle. The pavement on the Stanton Road ends at the corner where the stagecoach station stood, and if you continue straight east on the sandy road over the hills and through the woods, you may get some idea of what it was like to travel by stagecoach in those early days. Three-and-a-half miles farther east you come to Wormwood P. O. in Grand Traverse County, which nobody now seems ever to have heard of.

Four miles farther on is the Northport-Newaygo state road, which dates back to the 1860s. It was a busy thoroughfare in those days, but except for the locals (some of whom drive like gangbusters), hardly anyone uses it today.

4
Sparr Has Only One Mall

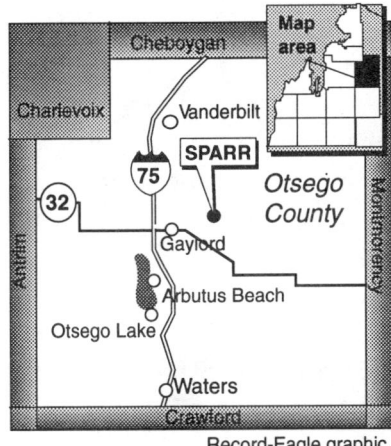

Record-Eagle graphic

Forget balloons, carousels, and acres of parked cars. The Sparr Mall isn't anything like that. For one thing, it's a good deal smaller, around twenty by thirty feet. But it has the same astonishing variety of merchandise you'd expect to find in a suburban shopping mall.

A partial inventory would read something like this: toothpicks and shoe laces, hunting knives and chain saws, beer and liquor and soda pop, canned goods and

The Sparr Mall.

coffee, hunting jackets and hunting caps, milk and ice cream, bread and doughnuts, jerkey and candy, sweat shirts and tee-shirts and overalls, motor oil and gasoline. And all of it is packed in an area not much bigger than Fibber McGee's legendary closet. (The gasoline pumps, of course, are outside.)

The store was built in 1925 by Ira House, who lives just across the road. Ira has spent most of his life in this little town, which lies a few miles north and east of Gaylord in Otsego County. He was born in Canada in 1902 and came to the area with his parents in 1913. Just recently he was guest of honor at a party celebrating his ninetieth birthday. He sold the store several years ago to his grandson, Don Boughner and his wife Phyllis, who, besides having a good sense of humor, are friendly and accommodating. They live above the store.

Sparr was named for pioneer Phillip Sparr, who settled here in 1873. But the town didn't get started until much later. Around 1913 the Boyne City Gaylord & Alpena came through the area on its way to Alpena. Initially, it consisted of a row of tarpaper shacks on each side of the road, a hotel and saloon, and a makeshift depot. A year or two later, Sparr had a post office with grocer John Hanley as its first postmaster. The Sparr school, built about the same time, doubled on Sundays for a church.

There was also a railroad switchyard and two spurs from Gaylord for loading 32-inch "chemical wood" to make alcohol, turpentine, and other wood by-products at a plant in that city. The logging in the area was done by Salling Hansen Lumber Company, with Dirk Schreur as boss of Camp 54. Charlie Sewell operated

The Marquardt school near Sparr.

Sparr in 1914. Hotel and saloon at left. Courtesy of Charlie Conn.

Railroad ticket to Sparr.

the sawmill at Sparr. Ira House's father, a blacksmith by trade, built and operated the Sparr smithy.

Potato farming was big business at Sparr in the early days. There were potato warehouses on three of the main four-corners. Art Wolfe's store, on the fourth corner, also housed the post office. He later built a "Soup House" which never operated as such but was taken over by Joe Dipzinski for a saloon, thereby perhaps filling a greater need.

Ira House remembers that as a teenager he'd make a daily trip to the saloon across the street from the warehouse to fetch a two-quart pail of draft beer for Art Wolfe, who was disabled. He says that in the 1930s the Sparr warehouses loaded over 156 carloads of potatoes in a single year; each car holding over 600 bushels.

The decline of the market for Michigan potatoes and the demise of the BCG & A Railroad spelled the beginning of the end of Sparr. The town is now reduced to just a few houses and, of course, the Sparr Mall, which surprisingly still shows abundant signs of life.

In addition to its relaxed and folksy atmosphere, the Mall has something you won't usually find at your average shopping center: a backyard wildlife enclosure. At present it houses two very big, but frolicsome black bears named Pokey and Smokey, a doe, and the biggest rabbit you ever saw in your life. It's a Flemish Giant, tipping the scales at sixteen pounds.

5
Waters and the Glass Bottle Fence

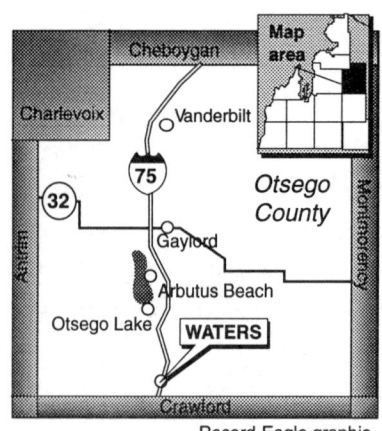

Record-Eagle graphic

Without its glass bottle fence Waters would have been just another ghost of a sawmill town on the Michigan Central Railroad tracks. The bottle fence made Waters famous.

The town was born in 1873 when the Wright-Wells Lumber Company built a sawmill on the north end of Bradford Lake twenty-seven miles south of Gaylord

Early days in Waters. Courtesy Waters Historical Society.

and began logging off the big pine forests in the area. In 1876 it was given a post office as Bradford Lake, and Charles H. Davis was its first postmaster. The lumber company also owned a hotel and a big general store that served a population of about one hundred

Papa Joe's tavern and gas station, 1935. Courtesy Waters Historical Society.

people. In 1885 the town was renamed Waters, probably because of the many lakes in the area and its emergence as summer resort country.

By that time the big timber was gone and the town languished with only a combined post office and store and a handful of people remaining. It was rejuvenated, however, in 1891 when lumberman Henry Stephens moved his operations north from St. Helens in Roscommon Country. Stephens had made a fortune there, cutting an estimated billion feet of virgin timber.

The remaining timber at Waters was soon depleted and the town went into a second decline—until around 1912, when Stephen's son, Henry, Jr., decided to make his home there and built a big two-story house on Main Street across from the depot.

Henry, Jr., who had inherited his father's fortune, was something of a playboy and world-traveler, but in 1914 or thereabouts he got a brilliant idea and embarked on what he considered a monumental project. He would build a memorial to the hard-working, hard-drinking lumberjacks who had helped make his father a millionaire and also contributed to his own life of ease.

He hired a cement contractor and over the next four years built a solid wall fence along the front of his property. The fence was made of glass bottles, thousands of them—beer bottles, whiskey bottles, milk bottles, all kinds of bottles–the only glass bottle fence in the world. It was 110 feet long, five feet high, and

World-famous glass bottle fence shortly after completion. Courtesy of Waters Historical Society.

it had a wrought-iron gate at the center. It was a wonder to behold.

To obtain the bottles Stephens hired local kids and paid them a penny each for all the bottles they could scrounge. It is said that some of them went back at night, swiped the bottles and sold them back to Stephens the next day. Stephens wasn't fooled but he was a good-natured sort of fellow (with plenty of money) and he paid up with a chuckle.

Close-up of a section of the fence.

Stephens took the trouble to explain to anyone who was interested that the fence was a tribute to the lumberjacks. But since the fence when finished was emblazoned with his name in letters two feet tall, it seems more like an ego-trip than anything else. (Oh, well; everybody wants to leave some kind of mark behind.)

The glass bottle fence became famous in the 1930s when it was featured in one of Ripley's *Believe It or Not* columns. It was also mentioned in Stewart Holbrook's popular *Holy Old Mackinaw*. It attracted thousands of tourists from all over the country. Unfortunately, it also attracted vandals who destroyed all but a section of it over the years.

The Stephens house burned down in 1935 and the land was donated to Otsego County for use as a firehouse and community hall. In 1970, the glass bottle fence was found to be on highway property and what was left of it was moved to the back of the lot.

There it lies today, sadly diminished, hardly noticed now by passersby.

6
Hallock Had a Gold Mine

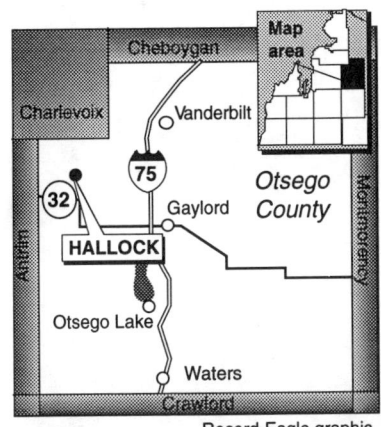
Record-Eagle graphic

Although gold has been mined successfully at several places in Michigan's Upper Peninsula, only two gold mines were ever recorded in lower Michigan. One was in Alcona County near Harrisville and is known as the "lost gold mine." The other is in Otsego County near the ghost town of Hallock, a few miles west of Gaylord, and several people know exactly where it is—especially Marvin Kelso, who grew up on the farm where the gold was found and had to skirt the holes with plow and harrow. He can show you the locations of both of the two mine shafts that were sunk in 1912. The shafts were filled in long ago and are now just shallow depressions in the ground.

Marvin is one of several members of the pioneer Kelso family who live on Hallock Road. His mother, Rhoda Kelso, owns the land where the gold was discovered. In the 1870s, her husband's grandfather, Andrew Kelso, was one of the original settlers of the long, green valley in the heart of Otsego's glacial hills.

Back then, the Houghton Lake-Harbor Springs Indian trail crossed the Kelso farm, and the Indians frequently stopped in for a drink of water and often were given a loaf of bread. The Kelsos liked the Indians and treated them well. One morning they got up to find a freshly-dressed deer hanging from a tree in the back yard.

The village of Hallock in 1920. Photo courtesy of Roy L. Dodge Historical Collection.

Hallock school 1895.

"It was the Indians' way of showing their appreciation," says Rhoda Kelso. "Other people didn't treat them nearly so well."

The village of Hallock owed its existence to the Boyne City Gaylord & Alpena Railroad which laid tracks through the valley on its way to Gaylord in 1906. It was named for Benjamin Hallock, who donated the land for the village. For many years he operated a big general store at the crossroads. His house is one of the only two original buildings still standing at Hallock. In addition to the store, Hallock had a post office (1906 to 1914), a depot (on legs because of occasional flooding), two other stores, a large Gleaners Hall, a church, and a school. Many of the local farmers worked in the nearby lumber camps during the winter.

Old house at Hallock.

In 1911, Charles Hatch found what looked like flakes of gold in an outwash bed of gravel on his farm. Without telling anybody for fear of ridicule, he sent samples to a friend out west, where gold fever was still high. The report came back saying that the sample assayed $3.50 worth of gold to the ton. Other samples—sixteen in all—averaged $2 per ton, a commercially profitable amount. Hatch broke the news to his neighbors and it spread like wildfire. On February 9, 1912, the *Otsego County Times & Herald* ran a story under the headline *Gold Mine Located in Otsego County*! It reported that Hatch could hardly wait until spring to start mining operations.

Details of the actual operations are scanty. Apparently, the Jackson Lansing & Saginaw Railroad, which had reached Gaylord in 1874 and still owned the mineral rights to the property, was involved. Two shafts were sunk: one on a hill north of the gravel bed, the other on the flat a quarter mile south. Both shafts were heavily shored up with timbers, but how deep they were remains a mystery. Marvin Kelso says that, in any case, the shafts were no deeper than 100 feet because that's the depth of the water table and the miners had no equipment to keep water from flooding the mine.

In another story that spring, the *Herald & Times* reported that mining operations were under way and great things were expected, but after that—nothing. Disappointingly, the story ends there. Apparently, gold wasn't found in sufficient quantities to make the digging profitable, and the mine was abandoned.

One of the old-timers at Hallock is skeptical. He says that probably there never was any gold, that it was all a scam by the JL & S Railroad to attract investors. "A productive gold mine would look pretty good on the balance sheet," he says.

But Marvin Kelso remembers that his grandmother showed him a little perfume bottle full of what she said was gold dust from the mine.

"Fool's gold," says the skeptic.

Somebody's always trying to spoil the fun.

7
Lonesome Pere Cheney

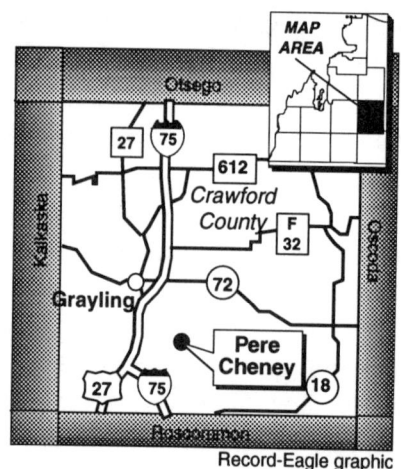
Record-Eagle graphic

Most Michigan ghost towns are lonesome places. But Pere Cheney must surely be one of the lonesomest of all. Except for a cemetery and a few holes in the ground, there's nothing left of it, not even a decent road—only a sandy two-track winding through the jack pine forest. As one old-timer put it: "Pere Cheney disappeared."

Yet, surprisingly, Pere Cheney (pronounced pair-a-shaney) was once a county seat.

The little lost village on the Michigan Central Railroad a few miles south of Grayling was the first settlement in Crawford County. It was settled around 1870 by lumberjacks and sawmill hands who followed the Jackson Lansing & Saginaw Railroad north into the big timber. It was named for G. M. "Papa" Cheney, who built the first sawmill and began lumbering operations there at that time.

In 1879, when Crawford County was being organized, Pere Cheney became the county seat—but not for long. The citizens of Grayling, more centrally located and arguably with a larger population, coveted the seat and persuaded the county supervisors to change it in their favor. In one of those "courthouse battles" that were common in those days, the Pere Cheney people put up a good fight but lost the war. A delegation from Grayling came down on the train and seized the court records. Later, Pere Cheney people claimed that Grayling had padded its population figures by registering lumberjacks and other itinerants on the voting rolls.

Despite the setback Pere Cheney continued to prosper. By 1881 it had a hotel, a big general store, three sawmills, a railroad depot, a school, and eighty people. Stewart Hutt became its first postmaster in 1874, and the post office operated until 1911.

All the same, the little village was doomed. By 1890 the big timber was gone, and people started to drift away. There was nothing to keep them. The light sandy soil was unfit for farming. By 1918 only eighteen people were left in Pere Cheney.

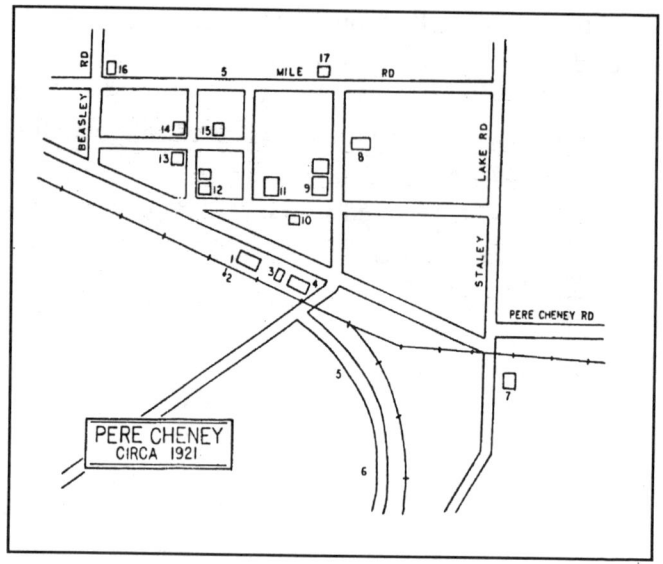

1. Boxcar—home for section foreman
2. Wooden arm for mail
3. Handcar
4. Boxcar—for freight, depot
5. Site of old sawmills
6. Cemetery
7. Goldsmith or Fox Farm
8. School
9. Hotel and barn
10. Richardson cabin, used by Corwin Family in 1921
11. General store
12. Dumphrey residence
13. Harley Williams residence
14. Ed Clover residence
15. Unknown residence
16. Egelston farm
17. Moon residence

(This map is based on the recollections of Everett E. Corwin of Beaver Creek Township, February 1990. It is not made to scale.)

Above: Pere Cheney cemetery.

Right: One of the few gravestones still intact at Pere Cheney.

Below: A heap of destroyed stones.

Disease had a lot to do with it. The turn of the century was hard on children. Smallpox, diptheria, and scarlet fever took a fearsome toll. In the terrible winter of 1893, for example, one Pere Cheney family lost five children to diptheria. That was calamity enough to dishearten the bravest survivor. It wasn't long before nothing was left of Pere Cheney except the cemetery, where many of its people are buried.

Their slumber, unfortunately, has not been peaceful. Over the years vandals have defaced, toppled or completely destroyed most of the gravestones. It is said that a man who later became sheriff of Crawford County was one of the worst offenders and that as a teenager he was seen driving around with a human skull in the back window of his car.

In 1989, the Grayling Veterans of Foreign Wars took upon themselves the task of cleaning up the cemetery. They removed the brush, cut the grass, and mended as many of the gravestones as they could. They also erected a sign, Pere Cheney Cemetery, and put up a flagpole.

Most of the children's graves are marked only by a fieldstone. Of the others, only these names are still legible: Johnson, William E. Nichols, Sewell, Frank Dompier, Theodore O'Dell, Charles & Nina Richardson and son Far R., and Barber.

8
Haring and the Shay Locomotive

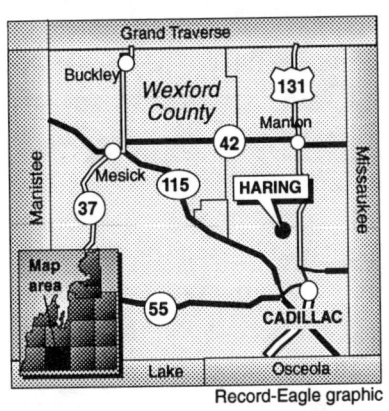
Record-Eagle graphic

Haring is a ghost town in Wexford County just north of Cadillac and is remembered chiefly because for many years it was the home of Ephraim Shay, inventor of the Shay railroad locomotive. The Shay engine made its inventor rich and famous.

Haring was one of many little lumbering settlements that sprang up along the Grand Rapids & Indiana Railroad, then making its way from Cadillac to

Ephaim Shay's prefab steel house at Harbor Springs.

Kalkaska and the streets of Mackinac. The village was settled in 1871 and Shay was one of the first arrivals. A young Civil War veteran, he had come to Michigan in 1865, freshly discharged from the Union Army medical corps. For a few years he ran a sawmill in Eaton County, then brought his family north to Haring, little more than a clearing in the big north woods.

Shay built the first general store and then a sawmill, and began cutting timber. The first postmaster at Haring was Hiram B. Wilcox in 1872, but Shay succeeded him after a year or two. The post office took its name from Haring Township; the railroad station was called Linden for several years.

In the early 1870s, the cost of transporting logs from stump to the sawmill had risen to $3.50 per thousand board feet—almost 75% of the total cost of production. To make matters worse, the bottom fell out of the lumber market in the Panic of 1873 and many Michigan lumbermen were going broke.

It was to meet this challenge that Shay, along with several others, began to experiment with a logging tramway to cut transportation costs. In 1873, he built a wooden tramway from the timber to his mill, using 4 x 4 pine timbers for ties and stringers and maple strips for rails. The logging cars were drawn by horses.

Shay locomotive working in the woods near Haring.

The horses were replaced in 1877 by a small locomotive, built largely by hand by Shay and William Crippen, who had a machine shop in Cadillac. During the next two years this prototype engine evolved into the gear-driven Shay engine, a product of Shay's inventive genius.

The Shay, produced under license by the Lima Locomotive & Machine Company of Lima Ohio, (and inevitably nicknamed "Limey") soon became known as the workhorse of the woods. What it lacked in speed

Right: Michigan Historic Site plaque at Cadillac City Park.

Below: Shay locomotive on display in Cadillac City Park.

it more than made up in traction, power, and versatility. It could pull as hard as a swayback mule (which it somewhat resembled) and turn in its own length like an Indian pony. It was the ideal machine for lumbering operations and, along with railroad logging in general, sounded the crack of doom for what was left of the great Michigan forests. What might have taken another fifty years by old-time logging methods was accomplished in ten by the logging railroads.

The essence of Shay's invention and its patent was the engine's limber drive-shaft. The shaft was made flexible by a clever arrangement of universal joints and sliding couplers. It provided a smooth, steady application of power which gave the locomotive its great traction and power. The Shay could go anywhere in the roughest kind of country, up and down gullies, dodging trees and stumps, taking the sharpest turns with ease. Many of the Shay locomotives are still in use around the world.

When Ephraim Shay and his family left Haring in 1888, he was already a rich man. He spent the rest of his life in Harbor Springs, where he continued to exercise his Edison-like genius by building the town's first waterworks, a prefabricated steel house of unusual hexagonal design, and a short-line scenic railroad. He died in 1916.

For all practical purposes, Haring died with Shay's departure. It lost its post office in 1889. Of the original houses and buildings, nothing remains except a hand-carved, hand-painted sign that marks the site of the Haring Township Hall. That, and the Haring Cemetery, are the only reminders of bygone days.

The cemetery at Haring.

9
Berryville Perished in a Fire

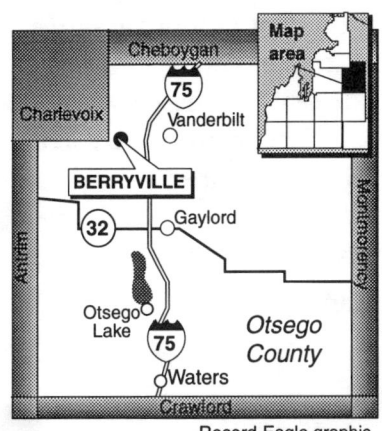

Record-Eagle graphic

In the little sawmill towns of northern Michigan's early lumbering days, what the settlers feared most was fire. A forest fire is an awesome thing: a raging inferno moving at express-train speed, consuming everything in its path, whole trees exploding in the intense heat even before the fire reaches them.

No wonder the villagers feared it most, living as they did in flimsy highly-combustible tarpaper shacks, without any means of fighting fire except a bucket brigade. A forest fire could wipe out a whole village in minutes. One such village was Berryville, in northwestern Otsego County near Vanderbilt.

Berryville was first settled in 1877, when Captain John G. Berry led a group of Civil War veterans and their families to the shores of a little jewel of a lake surrounded by steep hills covered with pine forest. They built a sawmill, a grist mill, a school, and a two-story general store. The sawmill was powered by damming the creek that runs from Berry Lake to Fitzek Lake. The top floor of the store was occupied by a Masonic Lodge, one of the first north of Bay City, with Captain Berry as its first master.

Berry also became the first postmaster when the town was awarded a post office in 1878. Berryville was then in Charlevoix county but later—along with Corwin Township—it was transferred to Otsego County. The Berry & Gagnir general store was de-

An abandoned house at Berryville.

The summer lodge on Bert Lake.

stroyed by fire in 1882, and Captain Berry moved to Vanderbilt to be nearer to the Jackson Saginaw & Lansing Railroad. There he opened a hardware store in partnership with a man named Skelton. The Masonic Lodge was moved to a hall over the store.

Berry, a man of many parts, also organized the first Otsego chapter of the Grand Army of the Republic and became first Commander of the General Harker Post No. 263, established in 1884. The last surviving member of G.A.R. Post 263 was Walter Caldwell, who died on his 94th birthday in 1931. Caldwell had been postmaster of Berryville until the office was closed in 1907.

1910 was a year of drought, and the woods around Berryville that summer were tinder dry. A fire, said to have been started by a logging railroad near Fitzek Lake and fanned by a strong south wind, spread rapidly through the pine slashings. By the time it reached Berryville it had become a crown fire, racing through the top foliage of the trees. It fell in its fury upon the villagers almost before they saw it coming.

One farm family, the Van Ettas, had just finished filling their barn with new-mown hay before going in for dinner at noon. After dinner they came out and found the barn on fire. Along with other nearby farmers and the villagers, they took refuge in the waters of Berry Lake and so survived the holocaust. There is no record of casualties.

But that was the end of Berryville. The fire also destroyed what was left of the forest and with it the livelihood of the Berryville people, most of whom moved to Vanderbilt. Nothing remains there now except a few ruined foundations.

The entire Berryville area was purchased in the early 1930s by a downstate family, who built a big rustic summer home on the site of the old lumber company's horse barn near the lake. Commendably, they also replanted the acreage to Norway and white pine, and the trees have grown so thick and tall that the place now must look the way it was before it was logged off more than a century ago. Many members of the family still summer there at the lodge.

10
Crawfords Quarry Got Swallowed Up

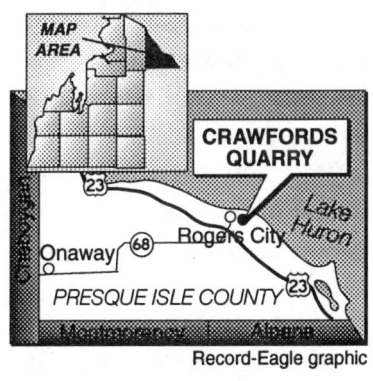

Record-Eagle graphic

Both timber and limestone gave birth to Crawfords Quarry, a ghost town on Lake Huron near Rogers City. Timber gave it birth and limestone rebirth.

Crawfords Quarry was the first permanent settlement in Presque Isle County (the name is French for "almost an island"). It was established by a remarkable Detroit family: Francis and Cynthia Crawford

The calcite limestone quarry, largest in the world.

and their three sons Leonard, Thomas, and Francis Jr. About 1860 they landed at a wooden dock in Presque Isle Harbor, and walked fourteen miles north to where they had taken title to thousands of acres of pine and hardwood forest on the lake shore. Crawford and his wife platted a village there which, not surprisingly, they named Crawford. It was given a post office under that name in 1864; Francis Crawford was the postmaster.

For a decade the Crawfords dominated business and political activities in the area. First they built a big dock and supplied cordwood to passing lake streamers and wood-burning tugs that hauled timber-laden schooners and barges to sawmills on Saginaw Bay. Later they built their own sawmill and shipped lumber, cedar posts, and other wood products downstate. They also cut some of the abundant limestone in the area and shipped it to Detroit for sale as build-

Right: Historic site plaque at the quarry.

Below: One of the earliest steam shovels at the quarry.

ing stone. Tom Crawford became county treasurer when Presque Isle County was first organized in 1870.

That same year saw the arrival on the scene of some serious challengers to the Crawford family domain. They were surveyors Albert Moliter and Fred Larke, who had formed a company with U.S. Commissioner of Surveying, William E. Rogers, to buy as much timberland in Presque Isle County as possible.

They tried to buy out the Crawfords but were turned down. So they bought the adjacent section to the north, laid out a village they called Rogers (it later became Rogers City), built a big sawmill, and brought in boatloads of German and Polish immigrants and French-Canadian lumbermen to settle the village, work at the mill, and cut the timber.

It wasn't long before Rogers was as big as Crawfords Quarry, and a great rivalry grew up between the two villages. Each claimed a right to the county seat, each built a courthouse, and for a time the county had two governments. That changed, however, in 1875, when the county was reorganized and Crawfords Quarry lost the courthouse battle to Rogers. Another loser in the battle was the contractor who built the courthouse at Crawfords Quarry: he never got paid for his work. The courthouse stood empty for years, a grim reminder of the village's blasted hopes.

Earlier, in the battle's final skirmish, Tom Crawford, charging fraud, refused to turn over the treasurer's books, and lawmen were sent down from Rogers to arrest him. To avoid capture he hid out in the woods for a day or two, then secretly boarded a tug one night, sailed away, and never returned.

By 1890 the big timber was gone and Crawfords Quarry became a ghost town. It got a new lease on life, however, in 1908, when it was discovered that the sixteen miles of lakeshore between Rogers City and Presque Isle Harbor contained a huge deposit of remarkably pure calcite, a primary source of lime. Now owned and operated by U.S. Steel, it has become the world's largest limestone quarry.

It was to Calcite (new post office name for Crawfords Quarry) that the ill-fated *Carl D. Bradley* was returning when it met with catastrophe. After delivering a load of limestone for the steel mills at Gary, Indiana, the big self-unloader of the Bradley fleet broke up and sank off Gull Island in the Beaver Island archipelago on November 18, 1958, with a loss of thirty-three lives.

The village of Crawfords Quarry now lies within the city limits of Rogers City. So, in the end, the village not only lost the courthouse, but also its identity—swallowed up by its old rival.

The *Carl D. Bradley*.

11
The Metz Tragedy

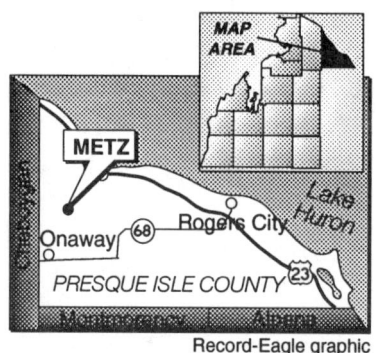
Record-Eagle graphic

The great forest fire on Michigan's Thumb in 1881 covered a wider area and the fire at Au Sable in 1911 destroyed more property. But in terms of human suffering and loss of life the forest fire that wiped out the town of Metz in Presque Isle County in 1908 was the worst in Michigan history.

Metz was settled in 1879 by mostly German immigrants. In a nostalgic mood, they named the township and the town after the city now in France but then a part of Germany. For the first twenty years they worked in the logging camps in winter and on their small farms the rest of the year. The Detroit & Mackinac Railroad came through in 1895 and gave the town a station. Robert Hoffman became the first postmaster that same year.

Although the big timber was depleted by 1900, Metz was firmly established as a shipping point for wood products and as a service center for the farming community. It had three general stores, a hotel and boarding house, a church, a blacksmith shop, several saloons, and a growing population.

It also had a rowdy reputation. The saloons were always crowded. They offered free lunch, and a man could spend the whole day and most of the night there, drinking and visiting with friends: barroom fights were a popular form of entertainment. All in all, Metz was

John Nowicki Hotel and Saloon.

Street scene in Metz before the fire. Courtesy of Metz Historical Society.

a boisterous, rough-and-tumble (some said sinful) kind of place. So when disaster struck the town on October 15, 1908, some people called it divine retribution—never mind that it was innocent women and children who suffered worst.

That day, a Thursday, was clear and mild with a strong fresh breeze blowing from the southwest. The kids went to school in light clothing and barefoot because of the summer-like weather. There was no early warning. By noon, however, people began to smell smoke and in the southwest the sky was dark with billowing clouds laced with dark red fire. The wind had risen to gale force. It soon became evident that Metz was in deadly peril. At two o'clock, the D & M station agent called headquarters at Tawas and asked for help. An engine was dispatched from Onaway, and a train was quickly made up at Metz. It consisted of eight or nine wooden cars and a steel gondola.

The problem now was getting people to board it. They were torn between fear of the fire and the anguish of parting with their cherished possessions. Not until the fire actually entered the town did many of them finally board the train, and it began its trip to Posen five miles to the east. For extra protection, most of the women and children, along with some of their household goods, were riding in the steel gondola. That turned out to be a ghastly mistake.

One of the survivors, station agent Jerry Annis, told the story: "We proceeded slowly, for with the fire close to the track in a number of places, the engineer feared spreading rails. At times, the fire was so hot ahead of us that we did not dare run through. We would back up until the rear of the train was near the last fire we had come through, whereupon the engi-

The burnt-up train at Nowicki's Siding. Courtesy of Metz Historical Society.

Above: Railroad officials inspect the tracks twisted by the fire. Courtesy of Metz Historical Society.

Left: Historic marker about the fire at Metz.

neer would open the throttle and we would go through. In this way we managed to get through the dangerous places along the track, until we arrived at blazing piles of wood products, railroad ties and cedar posts, at Norwicki's Siding."

"The engineer stopped, as before, tried to back up so as to make a dash through, but the fire had already closed behind us. It was no use, so with the throttle wide open he tried to go ahead. The engine and the gondola stopped right between the burning piles. Conductor Kinville cried out, 'Get out! Get out!'

"I got my wife and baby out, but we could not do a thing to help the women and children in the gondola .... Every car was on fire at once. Those who got out dashed into the ditch, and finally groped and crawled to a small open field filled with stumps. The stumps

Twisted and melted wreckage from the train. Courtesy of Metz Historical Society.

were blazing but we lay down between them. We dug away the top dirt and ashes with our hands and held our faces to the earth. The air was fearful, breathing was difficult, and a man could not walk far and live."

Sixteen people, mostly women and children, died at Norwicki's Siding. Scores of others in the township were maimed or seriously burned. Relief supplies poured in from all over the state, and the Red Cross built a number of 12' x 14' shacks to shelter homeless people through the winter. Later, one or two of the buildings and some of the houses at Metz were rebuilt, but the town never really recovered from the holocaust. Ironically, the only ongoing business now is a saloon.

The only ongoing business in Metz today is this saloon, built in 1912.

12
Alcona and the Log Rafts

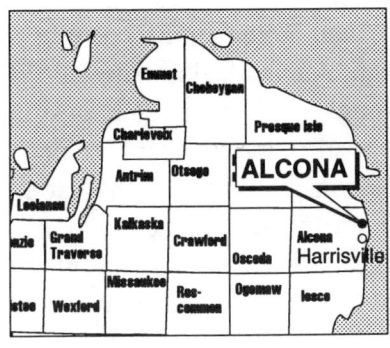

Alcona, a ghost town in Alcona County, went from birth to ghost in three stages—all within a matter of some thirty years. From 1858 to 1865 it was a fishing town; until 1885 a logging town; and now a ghost town.

Alcona lies on the shores of Lake Huron in Haynes Township seven miles north of Harrisville. It was first settled about 1858 by a Canadian-born commercial fisherman named William Hill. He called it "The Cove," and people called him the "Commodore of The Cove." Other fishermen and their families followed him, but not until ten years later was the settlement big enough to qualify for a post office. It was renamed Alcona, after the county, which had been given its Indian name by Henry Schoolcraft. (It is said to mean "beautiful plain," but one must be careful about Schoolcraft's Indian names.) Bryant S. Lagrange became its first postmaster on January 9, 1867.

By that time, the harvesting of the great stands of pine along the Lake Huron lakeshore was in full swing, and Alcona had become a busy logging town. It had two hotels, two general stores, a saloon, a large lumbermen's supply warehouse, a harness and blacksmith shop, boat docks, and more than 250 people.

Surprisingly, though, Alcona had no sawmill of any size (though its shingle mills were the largest in the country) and no railroad: the Detroit & Mackinac Railroad didn't reach Alcona until around 1895, long after all the big timber was gone. So, lacking a mill and a railroad, the logging company—Alger Smith & Company—had to move its logs downstate on Lake Huron and some of the logs were shipped on schooners, some on barges towed by tugboats. Great numbers were transported in huge log rafts. Log rafting has been carried on in other places in Michigan and around the country, but never on such a grand scale as was done in the Saginaw Bay area and Port Huron in the 1850s, '60s and '70s.

The operation was known as "watering the timber." Logs were moved from the woods to the lakeshore by horse-drawn sleighs, big logging wheels,

Above: The lighthouse at Sturgeon Point near Alcona was built in 1869.

Right: The rudder of the *Marine City* on display at Sturgeon Point lighthouse. The burned-out hulk of the ship lies offshore between Alcona and Sturgeon Point.

and, later by logging railroad. At the water's edge they were piled on skids—and there was a mile of logs on skids along the lake at Alcona.

When conditions were favorable—and this was only in June, July, and August when the weather is fairly predictable—the logs were dumped into the bay and herded by the rafting crews with pike poles into hollow squares, or booms, made of long timbers chained together. The booms were then towed by specially-trained horses to the anchored rafting point two miles out in the lake—starting out in shallow water and swimming the last leg with a drover astride one of the horses in the team. This work could only be done in perfectly calm weather, and the crews often worked day and night while the rafts were being built.

Alcona's only surviving building, once a grocery store.

At the rafting area the logs were turned over to the expert raftsmen—cat-footed, cork-booted men who worked on the slippery, bobbing pine logs as nimbly as if on dry land. They bored a hole through the end of each log with a hand auger, then strung the logs together with chains made fast to the boom logs on the sides of the square. This was a crib, and forty-eight of these cribs—six feet wide and eight feet long—comprised a raft. The tugboat hooked a line to the raft, and the long slow journey down the lake began, the long narrow string of logs trailing the tugboat like a snake.

The tug *Vulcan* was hauling such a raft on Sunday, August 28, 1880, when her captain spotted the steamer *Marine City* on fire off Sturgeon Point. He cast off the towline and hurried to the rescue. Along with another tug, the steamer *Metropolis* and the lifesaving crew at the Sturgeon Point Lighthouse, the *Vulcan* helped save the lives of most of the *Marine City's* passengers and crew.

Alcona lost its post office in 1903. By 1933 its population was down to one. He was a tall, lean, leathery man of seventy years of age named Newton Edwards, and he had been elected mayor of the town back in the 1880s. In the logging days he had worked as a harness-maker on the big logging wheels. When asked why he still hung around the town after everybody else was gone, he said, well, somebody had to keep an eye on things, and as mayor he figured it was up to him.

13
Potts-McKinley and Mr. Davis

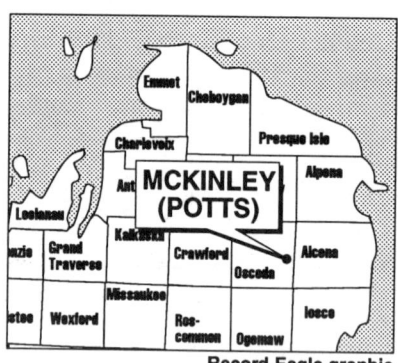
Record-Eagle graphic

Seeing it now, you'd find it hard to believe that McKinley was once the largest town in Oscoda County—not only the largest then, but the largest ever. Mio, the county seat, has about 1,500 people today. McKinley, in its heyday, had 2,000 people.

McKinley, a ghost town on the Au Sable River twelve miles east of Mio, was both a logging town and a logging railroad town. It was ideally situated for both purposes. To its central location in the heart of the county's timberland, the big pine logs were brought in from all directions by the many branches of the Au Sable & Northwestern Railroad, then rafted down the river to the mills at Oscoda and Au Sable. This was logging at its most efficient, and, environmentally speaking (which nobody in those days gave any thought), most devastating. At their peak in 1890, the Oscoda-Au Sable mills cut an astounding 324,503,531 feet of lumber.

The town got its start in 1884 when the Albert Potts Lumber & Salt Company of Au Sable started cutting timber in the area and made its headquarters there. In 1887, they built a narrow-gauge railroad from the town to Russell in Alcona County. The first engines, cars, and rails were floated on rafts down the river from Grayling. The rafts were then dismantled and the material was used to build a company hospital.

The town was named Potts and was awarded a post office in 1888. Jeremiah Hunt, an engineer on the logging railroad, became the first postmaster. The company operated twelve Shay engines on its branch lines.

Potts grew by leaps and bounds. In 1890, it had two hotels, two general stores, and a large company store, two drugstores, five saloons, a church, and a school. It also had an escape-proof jail made of 2 x 4s spiked together and covered inside and out with

The AuSable River near McKinley.

hardwood boards. Its only window was so small that a man couldn't even get his head through.

But the company overreached itself in 1890, when it tried to extend the railroad to Oscoda, and went bankrupt. Its interests were taken over in 1891 by the Henry M. Loud Company of Oscoda and Au Sable. They finished the railroad and built other branches into all parts of Oscoda County and even down into Ogemaw County. It was from 1891 to 1900, under the supervision of the Loud Company, that the town experienced its greatest growth and prosperity. In 1892, it was renamed McKinley, in honor of the sitting U.S. President.

In 1899, however, the company's engine shop, round house, and railroad repair shops were destroyed by fire. It was said to have been caused by a tipsy night watchman, who fell asleep and kicked over a torch at his feet. When Loud heard the extent of the damages, he decided not to rebuild at McKinley and transferred his logging railroad headquarters to Oscoda. By that time, most of the timber in Oscoda County was gone anyway. With the loss of its main industry, the town went into rapid decline, and its people began to move away. Some of the buildings, including the Loud company store, the depot and the jail, were moved to Comins, a growing community on the newly arrived Au Sable & Northwestern Railroad.

Among the few who remained was one of the town's most notable citizens, a black man named George Davis. Davis had worked in the lumbercamps as a cook. During the spring drives he transferred his kitchen to a kind of raft known as a "wanigan" and followed the rivermen on their long journey downriver to Oscoda. His was the first black family in Oscoda County.

Davis and his wife Isabell had three daughters and a son. One of the daughters was born disabled and died young. Daughters Cora and Emma moved to Bay City, married and raised families. In a tragic accident, son Jimmie drowned in the waters of the Au Sable River. Legend has it that he fell off the bridge at Mio or off the wanigan on a spring drive, and that his body was never found. His father built a cabin on a bend in the river still known as Davis Point and remained there until he died, hoping that his boy's body would be found.

It's a touching story, and there's only one thing wrong with it. It isn't true. A member of the Davis family in Bay City set the record straight several years ago. Jimmie was drowned in 1900, miles downriver in

George Davis and his family. Courtesy of Montmorency Historical Society.

Iosco County. His body was found on the river bank near the Lumberman's Monument on the backwaters of Cooke Dam, and was buried where it was found. George Davis did build a cabin on the river at Davis Point and lived there until he died in 1911. Isabell died in 1913. Together with the daughter who died young, they are buried in a lonesome little graveyard known as Comins Cemetery. It lies on a woods trail just north of the river near Cumins Flats. Three headstones mark their graves.

McKinley today is a collection of summer cottages, one small store, and few if any, year-around residents.

Right: The cottage resident has put up this sign.

Below: The McKinley Inn has been closed for years.

14
The "Lost" Gold Mine of Harrisville

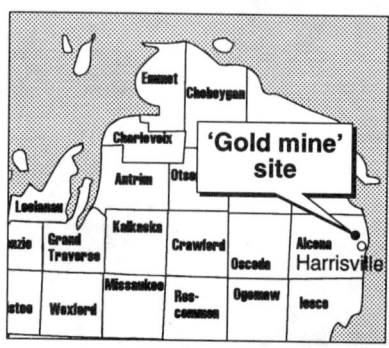

Roy Dodge first told the story of the lost gold mine of Harrisville in 1970 in an article for the *Bay City Times*. Later he included it in one of his books on Michigan ghost towns. Dodge got the story from a Harrison, Michigan, man named Frank Jozwiak. Jozwiak got it from his father, John Jozwiak, who was marginally involved in the venture.

According to Jozwiak—via Roy Dodge—gold was discovered in 1912 on the 40-acre Fleming farm in Haynes Township, Alcona County, seven miles north of Harrisville. The Fleming brothers, Thomas and Albert, made the discovery while engaged in digging a water well. At a depth of around twenty feet they found a gold nugget and forthwith abandoned the search for water.

The Flemings kept the discovery secret for several months while they organized a stock company to develop the mine. Called the Haynes Mining and Development Company, it was capitalized at $40,000 and nine members of the Fleming family were the chief stockholders. Gold mine stock certificates were offered to the general public at $25 a share. John Jozwiak, a Harrisville businessman and promoter, apparently helped the Flemings organize the company and sell the stock.

Meanwhile, mining operations at the farm went forward with vigor. In April 1913, the *Alcona County Review* reported that a large shaft was being sunk and

The Alcona County gold mine as it looked in 1913.
Courtesy of Roy L. Dodge Historical Collection.

hopes were high. The shaft had already reached a depth of seventy-five feet in blue clay and was going down at the rate of eight or nine feet per day. The miners were having some difficulty with water seepage, but pumping equipment had been ordered and was expected any day. Several weeks later, the miners found another gold nugget. At that point, however, tragedy intervened. The steam-operated mining equipment blew up, killing four men. The mine filled with water and was abandoned.

Jozwiak had another story his father told him. An old man living on a nearby creek (part of the Black River) made a fortune hauling black dirt from the creek to his shack during the summer and panning it for gold during the winter. (It would seem that summer was the best time to pan for gold and the creek the best place; but, never mind, that's how the story goes.) Jozwiak also showed Dodge a deed to the property, sold by the Flemings to his father, John. Its legal description is: forty acres of the northwest quarter of the southeast quarter of Section 8, Township 27, Range 9 East. Jozwiak said he had visited the property in 1969 and searched for the mine but was unsuccessful. In his 1970 story Dodge reported that, as of that date, the site of the mine was still a mystery.

Essentially, that was the story told by Frank Jozwiak to Roy Dodge. The reality, however, is somewhat different. According to Alcona County Register of Deeds Doris Gauthier, who has made a study of the matter, the Fleming brothers did indeed produce two

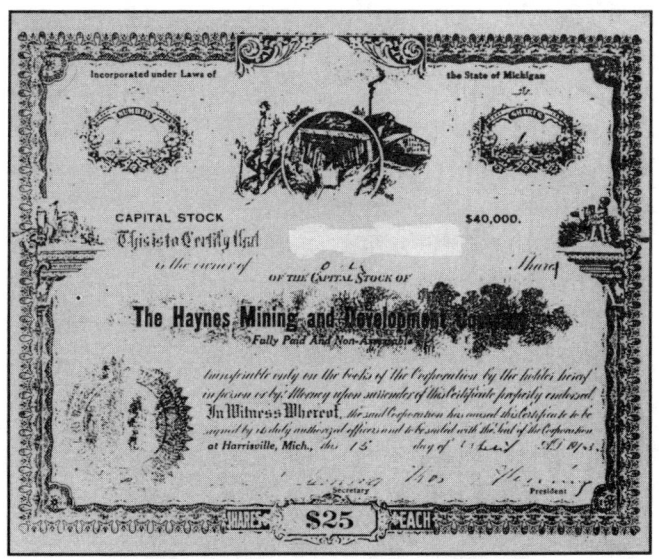

The gold mine stock certificate issued by the Haynes Company in 1913.

gold nuggets allegedly found in the mine. (It may or may not be significant that one of the brothers had visited Alaska some time previously.) The mining company was organized, a shaft was sunk, and great numbers of stock certificates were sold.

But there is no documentary evidence that the mine ever blew up or that anyone was killed: no newspaper story, no courthouse record. Indeed, Cora Sayers, who died in 1991 at the age of 99, remembered what happened. As a young girl she was baby-sitting at the Fleming house at the time of the explosion and she saw a man throw something in the direction of the mine, heard an explosion, and concluded later that it was a stick of dynamite.

The old man at the creek who got rich panning gold is sheer fantasy, one of the many rumors making the rounds in later years. The property that the elder Jozwiak bought from the Fleming is in Section 8, while the mining property is in Section 10. No wonder Frank Jozwiak couldn't find it.

The site of the mine has never been a mystery. Over the years the present owners of the property used the 20-foot-deep hole for dumping trash. (Their house, however, was torn down years ago; they live in Harrisville now, and the Fleming farm is vacant.)

The gold mine shaft as it looks today.

So much for the "lost" gold mine of Alcona County. Roy Dodge later acknowledged that he had been hoodwinked by Jozwiak's story. It seems clear now that the Flemings salted the mine, sold the stock, and pocketed the money. As usually happens in such typical gold-mine scams, the promoters got the gold and the investors got the shaft.

15
Pearl Harbor Made Mikado Mad

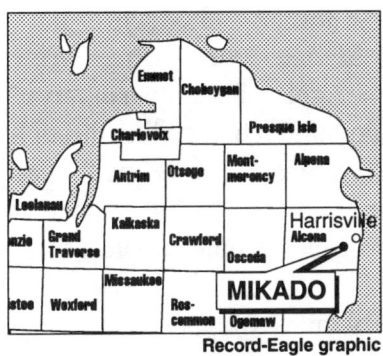
Record-Eagle graphic

The people of Mikado were hopping mad. It was Sunday, December 7, 1941, and the Japanese had just bombed Pearl Harbor. Like most of their countrymen, the villagers were outraged. Suddenly, Mikado, the name of their village was hateful. They wanted to change it. Anything Japanese had become anathema to them.

Mikado, a ghost town in southern Alcona County, owed its entire existence to the enterprise of one remarkable young man. Canadian-born Daniel Bruce emmigrated with his parents from Ontario to Huron County in 1865. He worked a year or two on the family farm and two years at a sawmill in Saginaw, then went north to work in the lumber camps in Alcona County as a surveyor.

Bruce found land that he liked in what is now Mikado Township. He bought a piece of it and decided to start a village. Much of the soil in the area was heavy with clay. He thought it would make good farmland and help sustain the village when the timber was gone.

He also thought it would be a great thing if he could bring a railroad to the village. In 1885, the Detroit and Mackinaw Railroad had begun to push north from Tawas into Alcona County. Bruce wrote the company offering free rights-of-way over his property if the railroad would build a branch line through the village. After several weeks, the company replied that a meeting of railroad officials was scheduled at Tawas next day and that they would be pleased to consider his proposal.

But Tawas was thirty miles away, and Bruce had no means of getting there except on foot. A heavy snow had fallen and he couldn't hire a livery rig. So he walked all night through the snow and arrived at Tawas at daybreak, just in time for the nine o'clock meeting.

At the meeting, Bruce raised his offer to include $360 cash, and that cinched the deal. The railroad agreed to make Bruceville a regular train stop, and the

Old Bailey School near Mikado is one of the few remaining one room log cabin schools in existence. It was built in 1894.

first train arrived on schedule in 1886. That same year, Bruce built a hotel for lumbermen with rooms for $1.50 a night. Other businesses, attracted by the railroad, soon followed.

So far, so good. But when it came to choosing a name for the post office, the authorities in Washington balked at Bruceville. They pointed out that Michigan already had a Bruce, and said that Bruceville would cause too much confusion. Finally, the Assistant Postmaster General, a Gilbert and Sullivan fan, decided to call the town Mikado, after the famous operetta spoofing the Japanese royal court (actually, by inference, a satire on the British royal court). It was playing to big audiences in Chicago at the time.

Although the villagers preferred Bruceville, in honor of the founder, and Mikado sounded outlandishly foreign to their ears, they soon got used to it—

Cemetery at Mikado.

especially after giving it their own homespun pronunciation. They called it Mi-KAY-do, instead of Mi-KAH-do, and so it is to this day.

As Dan Bruce had foreseen, the Mikado area proved to be excellent farmland, and the town became an important farming center. In 1901, in addition to the Bruce Hotel, it had two general stores, a cheese factory, a blacksmith shop and farm implement store, a church, a railroad depot and sixty people.

In 1920, it suffered a temporary setback when the Mikado branch of the D & M Railroad was abandoned; but by 1931 the population had more than doubled since 1901, and Mikado had more than a dozen businesses, including a bank and a grain elevator.

But the Great Depression took its toll. The population declined and some of the businesses went broke. And then came Pearl Harbor. The townspeople clamored for a name change, and the township board voted to change the name to "Marian Clare," in honor of the singing star who had made her first hit in the operetta, the *Mikado*. The movement got national publicity in *Life* magazine and on the radio. The *Chicago Tribune* and radio station WGN offered to build a park with a bandstand in Mikado if the singer's name was chosen. The matter was put up for a township vote.

Before the vote was taken, however, Marian Clare wired each member of the township board that she was withdrawing her name in favor of "MacArthur" or "Colin Kelley," which she understood were being considered. In the end, the movement lost steam and the matter was quietly dropped. And the ghost town and township still bear the name of the Emperor of Japan.

16
The Lost City of Damon

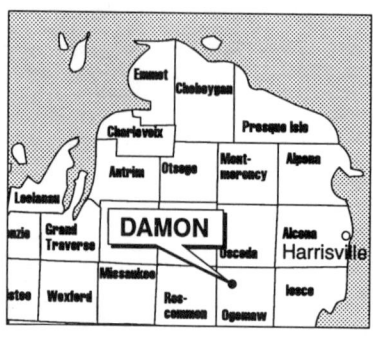

The lost city of Damon was never a city and was never really lost. It was given the title by James Oliver Curwood, a popular writer of outdoor fiction in the early 1900s. Damon is a ghost town in northwestern Ogemaw County near Rose City.

Owosso-born Curwood visited the place in 1911—when Damon was already a ghost town—and he used it as background for his romantic novel, *Green Timber*, which was published after his death in 1927. Curwood completed only one hundred pages before he died, and his publishers hired another writer to finish the book.

Green Timber opens with Curwood's heroine, Hilga, who still lives in Damon, telling its story to newcomers Allan and his little daughter Petrie, in what obviously sets the stage for a budding romance.

"Damon was named after one of the partners, Phineas Damon, of the firm known as Cutting and Damon," she says. "They had a mill near Beaver Lake, now a flag-stop on the Michigan Central between West Branch and St. Helen."

All of which is true, except that Curwood exercised his privilege as a novelist by changing George G. Damon's first name to Phineas.

In 1875, Cutting and Damon moved its lumbering operations north from Beaver Lake and established a village on the old State Road from West Branch to Luzerne. George himself took up residence for a while, and the town was named after him.

Pine logs were hauled from Damon on a tote road to the banking grounds at Rose City, then floated down Houghton Creek and Rifle River to the booming grounds on Saginaw Bay. Later, a narrow-gauge logging railroad was built north of Damon, and the first engine was skidded up from Beaver Lake, an operation that took six days.

According to legend, a strange accident befell the railroad. While it was being built, cars loaded with steel rails were moved to the end of the track, more track was built and the cars moved on. One night after the crew quit work, two cars loaded with rails sank in a quicksand bog and disappeared. Old timers say that the cars are still there, at the bottom of a pond.

The grocery store and the barn today at Damon.

Business interests at Damon were taken over by Davison Brothers, originally from Lapeer. They had a store at Beaver Lake and later on at McKinley and Mio in Oscoda County. Frank Davison built a big log general store at Damon, and a two-story, 17-room hotel with a livery stable for twenty-four horses. All supplies had to come up from Beaver Lake, and it took twelve teams making two trips a day to supply the store and others along the way. Andrew Jackson Warner was one of the stagecoach drivers. He drove an 18-passenger stage on the Damon-Beaver Lake and the Damon-Mio runs, making a round trip each day. Later, he ran the hotel for the Davisons.

One day in the summer of 1893, Cutting and Damon closed down all their mills at once and moved their operations to Texas. Davison Brothers soon followed suit, after selling the town of Damon to A. J. Warner for $350—including the hotel, store, most of the other buildings and tenant houses, and 326 acres. Warner and his family continued to live at Damon and they operated the store until 1906. In 1916 they sold out to a small lumbering company that cut the remaining hardwood, and moved to Gratiot County. By that time most of the buildings and houses had been torn down or moved away, and the town was abandoned.

In 1945, Warner's son Dewey, who had been born at the Damon Hotel, bought back some of the acreage. He and his wife operated a fishing and hunting lodge, and a small store, until 1957, when they sold the place to a downstate couple who started a dude ranch. It lasted only a few years after they learned how much it cost to winter twenty horses.

Green Timber made Damon famous overnight. Hundreds of people visited the ghost town each summer during the 1930s. Their interest in the place was enhanced by the many small signs showing the location of all the old buildings and mills—each with a small sketch of the building itself. They were painted during the Great Depression by an artist at nearby CCC Camp Ogemaw.

But these have long since disappeared, and there isn't much left to see. Few people read James Oliver Curwood any more, and hardly anybody visits the lost city of Damon.

17
Fouch: Where Boats and Railroad Met

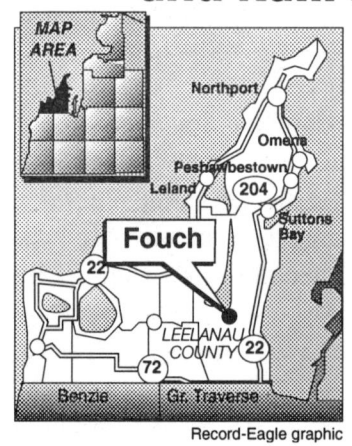

Record-Eagle graphic

Believe it or not, Fouch was once a transportation center. Sometime in the early 1860s, a black man named Smith came to the south end of Lake Leelanau (then called Carp Lake) and built a small dock. This was handy for early settlers on the lake: they could come down the lake in small boats or canoes, tie up at the dock, and walk to Traverse City for provisions, eight miles away. The place soon became known as Smith's Landing.

Unfortunately, that's all we know about Smith. He has vanished into the mist, leaving behind only his ubiquitous family name and the fact that he was black.

In 1866, 21-year-old John R. Fouch and his wife Hannah came from Ohio and homesteaded 260 acres in Elmwood Township and in what later became Solon Township. The acreage included Smith's Landing and considerably more of the lakeshore.

Even at that tender age Fouch was a Civil War veteran. He enlisted in the Union Army at age nineteen, and he served exactly one hundred days until the war ended in 1865. He'd been brought up on a farm, and before long he turned most of his Leelanau County acreage into profitable farmland.

Fouch also built a small summer resort at Smith's Landing, one of the first on the lake. When the Manistee and Northeastern Railroad came through from Solon to Traverse City in 1892, he built a station and acquired a post office, both in his name. He became the first postmaster in 1893. The office was closed in 1895, but was restored in 1905, with Mrs. Kate V. Herbert as postmistress.

The railroad station was unique. Most of the M & NE stations were built pretty much to the same pattern: they all looked alike. Fouch was different. It consisted of two small buildings—passenger depot and freight office—under one roof.

From the open space between them Fouch built a tramway down the gentle slope to the dock and installed a small flatcar for transporting baggage and

Carp Lake House, later called Hotel Wisteria. The sign on the gable appears to have been dubbed in by the photographer, who left the "E" off the end of "House." Courtesy of the Julius Petertyl Collection.

freight to the small steamers that plied the lake between Fouch and Leland, with stops along the shore. It was a nifty arrangement.

The first of these commercial passenger boats was the little steamer *Sally*. Captained by Morgan Cummings, she began making one round trip daily between Leland and Fouch in the spring of 1892. Leelanau County people could take *Sally* and meet the M & NE morning train at Fouch, then spend seven hours in Traverse City and catch *Sally* homeward bound in the late afternoon. It was a lot faster and more convenient than driving to Traverse City in a horse-

and-buggy or wagon. Two other boats, the *Tiger* and *Leelanau*, replaced *Sally*, and *Leelanau* operated until 1929. By that time, the automobile was beginning to displace both boats and railroads. The branch line of the M & NE from Solon to Traverse City was abandoned in 1934.

In 1905 Fouch built a resort hotel on the slope between the railroad and Fouch Road and called it Carp Lake House. The name was later changed to Hotel Wisteria. It burned down in 1915 and was never replaced.

In 1927 Daniel and Julia Perrin came up from Detroit and bought the place from the Fouchs—they had camped there with sons Earl and Dan for several

The steamer *Tiger* at Fouch Landing, showing the tramway from the railroad station. Courtesy of the Julius Petertyl Collection.

The Fouch cemetery.

summers. They filled in some of the wetland and established a cabin colony, which they called Perrin's Landing. It was taken over later by Earl and his wife Dorothy, who built a log lodge, a store, and sixteen more cabins—including one that floated offshore on oil drums. It was great for fishing and swimming, but when the wind came up, the booming of the waves against the oil drums drove the occupants ashore for lack of sleep.

Earl was a man of legendary strength. It was said he could hoist a 50-gallon oil drum to his back and walk away with it. Nobody ever beat him in Indian wrestling. Enormously likable, gentle with people and animals, he was a great fisherman and hunter. Small boys idolized him and spent hours of practice learning how to whistle through their teeth as Earl did.

The Perrins sold the resort in 1987 to Larry and Pat Walski of Grand Rapids. It is still in operation.

A small, untended burial ground known as Fouch Cemetery lies on Fouch Road just east of Perrin's Landing. Few people know of its existence. It belongs in Solon Township but got left in Elmwood Township when Solon was created in 1871. The cemetery contains the grave of John Fouch's first wife, Hannah, who died in 1875, and of a baby named Willy. Other names on the headstones of the half dozen graves are Fox and Thacker.

18
Manistee County's "Mystery House"

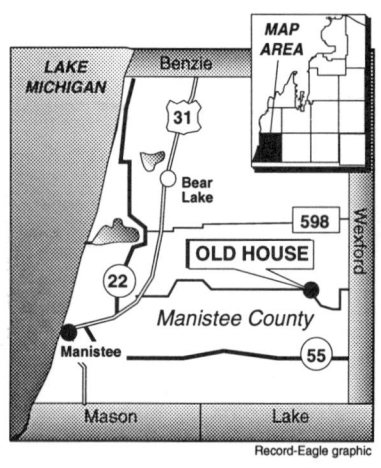

In 1832, when all of Michigan north of Grand Rapids was an unbroken wilderness peopled only by Indians and a few white missionaries, a party of men from Massachusetts arrived by schooner at the mouth of the Manistee River. They debarked, unloaded their gear and provisions, and ascended the river in small boats to Section 36, Town 22 North,

Range 14 West, a distance of some thirty river miles. Here they set up camp and proceeded to get out square timbers for a blockhouse and a dam for the operation of a sawmill.

The whole expedition is shrouded in mystery. Details are scanty. We don't know where in Massachusetts they came from. We don't know how many men there were. We don't know any of their names. By deduction it seems reasonable to assume that the last leg of their journey was from Sault Ste. Marie or the Straits of Mackinac in a sailing vessel skippered by a Captain Humphrey, who in later years sailed one of the boats of the Englemann Line, which plied the eastern shore of Lake Michigan between Manistee and Traverse City in the 1860s and '70s.

We do know that they built the blockhouse, a very substantial building that incorporated some of the architectural features of the Greek Revival style, which was becoming popular on the eastern seaboard in those days. The river site was ideal for building a dam—indeed, it was the exact spot where many years later the first power dam on the river was built by Consumers Power Company. But soon after these men started building their dam, the local Indians assembled and by "threatening gestures" (as the story goes) made it plain that they wanted them gone.

The Indians were mostly Chippewa, and they were legally (and every other way) in the right. The Manistee River valley was part of their sacred homeland. In the eyes of the Indians, these men from Massachusetts were intruders and trespassers. In their eyes, this was a bunch of crazy white men running around, cutting down trees, scaring off the game, and raising hob with the habitat. They wanted them out of there, and were prepared to move them out by force if necessary.

The men from Massachusetts apparently got the message. They packed up and went back down the river, never to return. Meanwhile (or perhaps later), Captain Humphrey returned with machinery for the mill. But he was unable to cross a sandbar at the mouth of the river, and for reasons unknown he unloaded the machinery and sailed away.

The Indians left the blockhouse untouched, and it stood empty for several years, the only mark of white civilization for many miles around, a wonder to behold. Later, a gang of counterfeiters moved in and began turning out batches of bogus greenbacks in relative security from the law—until one day a U.S. surveyor happened to stumble in on them, and, their cover blown, they hastily decamped and set up shop somewhere else. (The surveyor was none other than A. S. Wadsworth, who founded the town of Elk Rapids in 1852.) Still later, the house was used as a logging shanty, a whiskey saloon, and a dwelling occupied by a family named Dixon.

The Dixons are a story in themselves. John William Dixon was born in Sheffield, England, in 1820, and came to this country in 1849, his wife Maria and a newborn son having died and been buried at sea. In Detroit he married an Indian woman named Eliza

Taylor, and together with John's three other children by Maria, they moved into the old house on the Manistee River about 1851. One of John's daughters married James Silverly in 1853, and their first child, James, was born in 1854, but died four or five days later and was buried near the old house.

On April 16, 1880 the *Manistee Independent* noted: "Mr. John Dixon, the pioneer lumberman of Manistee County, and who is now more than 60 years of age, was made happy last Thursday by the advent of a ten-pound boy in his family. Mr. D. is now father and grandfather of 73 living children." John died in 1893.

Over the years, the old blockhouse became a familiar landmark in Manistee County, and was known far and wide as the Old House. It stood on a high bank on the north side of the Manistee River until some time in the 1860s or early 70s, and then it disappeared—whether by fire or demolition is not known. In 1876, Manistee historian General Byron M. Cutcheon wrote that it "was still standing until a few years ago," but had nothing to say about what happened to it.

The site now overlooks Tippy Dam, which was built by Consumers Power Company in 1918. On the south side of the river, a three-mile stretch of dirt road that leads to it from the west is still identified on county maps as Old House Road. But now only the road and the mystery remain.

19
Meredith Was a Wicked Town

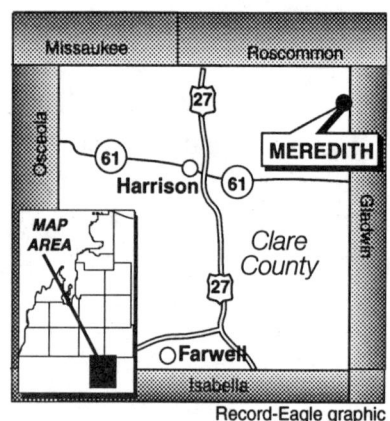

Record-Eagle graphic

Most Michigan ghost towns started with a sawmill or a railroad or a mine. Meredith in Clare County was different. It started with a saloon. Maybe that's why people said it was doomed from the start.

In the 1880s Meredith was known far and wide as SIN CITY, USA. Its business was whiskey and illicit sex. Its trademark was sudden violence and death. One resident claimed that he counted 27½ fights on the streets in a single afternoon.

When asked to explain the one-half fight, he said, "A feller came up to me and said he could lick any man in Clare County. I said that was taking in a lot of territory and knocked him cold with one punch to the jaw. That was the half of a fight."

Pine timbering in Clare County reached a peak in the late 1870s and '80s. There were fifty lumber camps in the northern townships and the woods were crawling with lumberjacks. But the nearest watering hole was in Harrison and that was a long way for a thirsty man to go for a drink. The town of Meredith got started when Thomas McClennon, a prosperous saloonkeeper in Saginaw, decided to take advantage of the situation.

In 1882, McClennon bought several hundred acres at the railhead of a branch line that the Flint and Pere Marquette Railroad had driven into the Franklin Township woods in 1881. There he built an elaborate saloon and hotel, which he named the Corrigan House after a conductor on the Meredith branch line. Completed in 1884, it stood three stories tall on a 45' x 150' foundation.

Other businesses soon followed. In 1883 Meredith consisted of one log house. By March of 1884, forty buildings were up and seventeen businesses established, including two general stores, two jewelry stores, a meat market, livery stable, sawmill, three restaurants and two saloons. Eventually Meredith had twelve saloons. Strategically situated on the line between Clare and Gladwin counties, it became the favorite watering hole for some 3,000 lumberjacks in the area.

The dining room of the Carey Brothers lumber camp near Meredith.

McClennon had the monopoly on booze. Not only did he supply the other saloons, but each lot in Meredith had the restriction that nobody except McClennon could sell whiskey or beer in Meredith without paying him a $400 annual fee in addition to the regular $300 license.

McClennon was a big man, intimidatingly strong, and only one man ever challenged him on this. Dewey Allen from Vernon Township leased a lot, erased the restriction, and sub-leased it to a Mount Pleasant saloon keeper by the name of O'Brien, who opened a tavern on it. As soon as he heard, McClennon boarded the next train for Meredith from his Saginaw home and gave O'Brien exactly one hour to get out of town. O'Brien emptied his shelves, packed his goods in a hired livery rig, and cleared the city limits with twelve minutes to spare. Nobody argued with Tom McClennon. McClennon was its founder, but the story of Meredith is basically the story of Jim Carr. Carr was one of Michigan history's worst scoundrels.

Born in New York state in 1855, Carr came to Clare County's north woods in 1878. After working three years in a lumber camp he turned up in Harrison seeking easier ways of making money than cutting down trees. In 1881, he formed an unholy alliance with a prostitute named Maggie Duncan which, while they disdained matrimony, nevertheless lasted until they died together a decade later.

That same year Carr built a combined saloon, dance hall, and brothel—with Maggie as madam—on a hill just outside Harrison. In two years he made so much money selling whiskey and women, rolling

An ink sketch of Jim Carr.

drunks, and cashing lumberjacks' time cards at a 25% discount that in 1884 he opened a branch saloon and "stockade" in Meredith, installing one of the Harrison girls as den mother.

By this time Carr had acquired a considerable reputation for murder, arson, and various other felonies. He was said to have been involved in the murder of at least three men, and that with two accomplices he had burned down a rival "stockade" near Harrison. One of his victims was a man who operated a bordello in Meredith before Carr got there and whom Carr couldn't persuade otherwise to leave town. Another was buried on the Meredith "stockade" premises under a dead horse. Investigators later dug up the horse

Stockade: Brothel owner Jim Carr hired women as prostitutes and allegedly murdered one of them.

but couldn't find the man. Carr was a mild, soft-spoken, medium-size man, quieter than a rattlesnake but just as deadly.

Jim Carr's big troubles began when he caused the death of Frankie Osborne, one of the girls at the Meredith "stockade." In retaliation for a flippant remark, Carr knocked the girl down using brass knuckles, kicked her, and then turning to his bouncer said, "Finish her off." The bouncer kicked her into insensibility; she died that night in her bed upstairs.

This brutal act was to be Carr's undoing. Up until that time, the law in Clare County had been practically invisible. But in 1884, a reform candidate, W. A. Burritt, was elected prosecuting attorney, and he vowed to get on Carr's case and put him behind bars. It took him two years to do it, hurdling such obstacles as hung juries, suborned witnesses and venal judges, but on January 21, 1886, Carr was sentenced to fifteen years in Jackson prison for murder. Maggie was also convicted of running a bawdy house and sentenced to a year in the Detroit House of Correction.

Both returned to Meredith in 1887, when Carr's conviction was overturned by the State Supreme Court on the grounds that it was based on inconclusive evidence. But Burritt continued to hound Carr with arrests and trials for arson, murder, and other crimes, and by 1890 Carr was virtually penniless after paying the fees of expensive Flint and Saginaw attorneys. His health, too, was broken by alcoholism and venereal disease.

On March 15, 1892, in a wretched little lumber shanty on an abandoned logging railroad south of Meredith, Jim and Maggie died within hours of each other. One of Carr's old lumberjack cronies, Lame Bob, who had been delegated by a doctor to look after them, got drunk and let the fire go out. When the doctor checked next morning, he found Jim dead on a straw pallet on the floor and Maggie nearly so on a couch covered with rags. Carr was only thirty-seven.

Like Sodom and Gomorrah, Meredith perished by fire. A series of conflagrations in the late 1890s, some of them deliberately set, destroyed the main buildings, and a huge brush fire around 1900 left all the rest in ashes.

20
Selkirk: A River Runs Through It

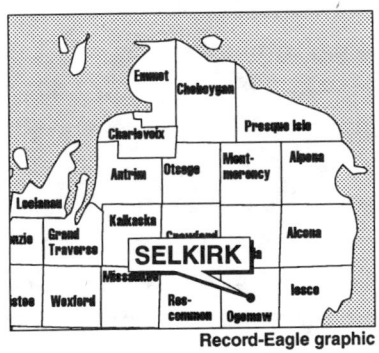
Record-Eagle graphic

It's a medium-size river, in most places not much bigger than a stream, and if you didn't know much about old-time logging operations, you'd wonder how in the world they ever got all those big pine logs down it. They did it, of course, by building a series of dams, one after another, down the river from Selkirk to Omer near Saginaw Bay.

It worked fine for white and Norway pine—"cork pine" the lumberjack called it because it floated so high in the water—but not so well for the heavier

The Rifle River runs through Ogemaw County and the ghost town of Selkirk.

hardwoods. But by the time the pine was gone and they began cutting the hardwoods, the logging railroad had replaced the river for transporting logs down to the mill.

The Rifle River is a clean clear cobblestone-bottom stream that flowed south through the center of Ogemaw County and through the ghost town of Selkirk, ten miles south and a little east of Rose City. Selkirk never had a railroad, but it was a staging area where the big pine logs were piled on skids in the winter and floated downriver in the spring. On Saginaw Bay they were gathered into huge rafts and hauled by tugboat across to the sawmills at Bay City.

In the early 1860s, lumbermen moved into Ogemaw County, traveling the tote road from the Bay City-Saginaw area, and began to harvest the great stands of virgin pine along the Rifle River. The town of Selkirk got its start in 1870, when the State Road (Old M-55) from Tawas to Manistee was completed. Like most other State Roads built during this period, it was a plank road: constructed of logs and planks covered with dirt and gravel. Even today you can feel the "corduroy" as you drive along it, especially on the hills. And once in a while one of the logs or planks may pop up in the gravel roads or even paved roads on hot days when the sun has softened the asphalt.

That same year, Bay City lumbermen Squires and Sterling built a hotel at Selkirk, and it became a stopping place for travelers on the State Road. They hired the Carascallen brothers, Roy and Herb, to run the hotel and a big general store. Selkirk was awarded a post office in 1887, and by 1900 it had acquired the usual complement of churches, a school, a blacksmith shop, a sawmill, saloons, and several hundred people.

The Quaker Church, built in 1903, is no longer being used.

The town began to fade with the end of lumbering. The soil, consisting mostly of light sandy glacial till, wasn't much good for farming; and after the automobile began to abbreviate distances, most people drove to Rose City or West Branch to do their shopping. The decline was slow but steady: Selkirk managed to hold onto its post office until 1955. Ironically, with almost everything else gone, the town has a small sawmill still in operation.

The Selkirk area was once the abode of an older people. Upstream and down along the river, and within a mile-and-a-half of the village, are four remarkable Indian earthworks.

Three of them are circular; one is a rectangle with an open side—archeologists believe that this one was never finished. The largest of the circular works is 314 feet long and 280 feet wide. The walls vary between two and five feet high, and the surrounding ditch

A section of the Indian earthworks at Selkirk.

The cemetery at Selkirk.

is between three and seven feet deep. Four causeways mark the entrances, which are just wide enough for two people to walk abreast.

The earthworks were a source of great curiosity to the early settlers. They called them "forts" and speculated that they had been built during the French and Indian War. Actually they are much older, having been radiocarbon dated to about 1300 AD plus or minus seven years. It is now believed that they were palisaded villages built by the Ottawa Indian people. Curiously, incidental digging by professional archeologists has produced only a few potshards and no stone weapons or tools. This seems to indicate that the villages were occupied most of the time by women and children while the men were off on extended trading or hunting trips. Like the Phoenicians of ancient times, the Ottawas were the travelers and traders of the Indian world.

The villages may have been an attempt by the Ottawas to colonize new territory. In any case, the villages were occupied for only a short time. After a century or two of relatively mild weather, Michigan's climate turned much colder around 1500 AD, and may have driven these people to seek warmer climates.

The Rifle River enclosures are among the most interesting of Indian earthworks that haven't been destroyed by pillagers or the plow. They lie within the confines of the Ogemaw State Forest and are definitely off limits to amateur archeologists. Look if you must, but please don't disturb.

21
Herron Had a Uranium Mine

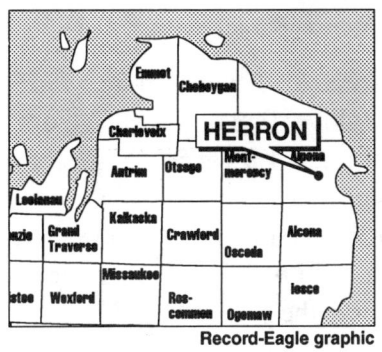
Record-Eagle graphic

At least three lower Michigan ghost towns had a gold mine, but only one had an uranium mine. On October 5, 1952, it blew up, killing five men.

The ghost town of Herron, twelve miles southwest of Alpena, was first called Frenchtown. It was settled by French Canadian loggers, who homesteaded small farms in the area toward the end of lumbering days in the late 1880s and '90s. One was Fred Herron, after whom the town was named—probably by the Boyne City Gaylord and Alpena Railroad, which came

All that's left of Herron today are the remnants of the Alex Domke general store and grain elevator.

through the area on its way to Alpena around 1915. Other early settlers were Oliver Prevo, Joseph Patnode, John Campeau, Alphonse LaBarge, Napoleon Cousineau, and Jay Napper.

In its heyday Herron had a boarding house, two general stores, two blacksmith shops, a grain elevator, and a sawmill. To serve the predominately Catholic population, masses for St. Rose Church were held in the upstairs of Prevo's Blacksmith Shop, as were card parties, dances, and other social activities. The Prevos, Oliver and Adelore, were musically inclined and provided fiddle and accordion music for weekend hoe-downs. The comparatively new St. Rose Church still holds services for the local farm community—but nobody lives in Herron any more: nobody, that is, except the St. Rose Church priest and his housekeeper.

Herron was granted a post office soon after the BCG & A Railroad came through. It was located in the general store of Alexander Martin, who had moved his family from Leer to Herron in 1918. Martin bought the store from L. N. View and moved it across the street from the St. Rose Church property. He became the town's first postmaster on October 5, 1920.

The uranium mine? Actually, it too started out as a gold mine. In 1928, a Chicago promoter named Charles Herriman engaged a local crew and sank a one hundred foot shaft on the Angus Morris property on the Taylor-Hawks Road just north of Herron, looking for gold. Why he chose this particular site is anybody's guess. Any geologist could have told him that the chances of finding gold in the limestone rock under Alpena County were practically zero. But maybe he was looking more for investors than for precious metal.

The covered shaft of the gold-uranium mine.

In any case, no gold was found, and the mine was abandoned after an explosion in the shaft wrecked a small building holding the mining machinery. One of the workmen lit a cigarette and tossed the lighted match into the shaft. There was a strange sputtering sound and somebody yelled: "Get out of here!" Everybody scattered; fortunately none of the four or five men and a little neighbor girl was injured in the blast.

Twenty-four years later, another Chicagoan named John Wilczynski leased the old gold mine from Angus Morris and deepened the shaft to 272 feet, looking for uranium. Again, any geologist could have told him that the chances of finding commercial quantities of uranium in the substrate limestone and shale were only a little better than zero. But like a lot of other people in the late 1940s and '50s who were tramping around the country with Geiger counters—particularly in Canada—Wilczynski had caught uranium fever.

On the night of October 5, 1952, Wilczynski and his crew of mostly Herron men were working the mine in a last minute effort to obtain additional rock samples before closing the mine for the winter. It was said that they were encouraged by finding uranium ore in previous samples. Two of the men, Sieghard Domke and his brother-in-law Ralph Chevalier, had descended in a cable car and were operating a pneumatic drill on a platform about 170 feet below the surface. Three others, John Wilczynski and brothers Bernard and Henry Domke, were working in support at the top of the shaft.

Another Chicagoan, John Pastruszka, was tending the diesel machinery in the powerhouse and tool shed nearby.

Suddenly there was a terrific explosion. Henry and Bernard Domke and John Wilczynski, who were near the edge of the shaft, were hurled into the air; their dismembered bodies were scattered in the surrounding fields. John Pastruszka was the lone survivor. He had been following Wilczynski to the shaft but turned back to check the fire in the work shed. The explosion blew him out the side of the building, but he suffered only minor injuries. The bodies of Seighard Domke and Ralph Chevalier were recovered from the mine two days later.

Investigators theorized that the explosion was caused by a spark from the pneumatic drill which ignited a pocket of gas or critical level of gas from seepage into the shaft. The tragedy was devastating to the little Herron community. The five men who were killed left twenty-six fatherless children.

Some Michigan maps show Herron on M-32 at the corner of Herron Road. But the original village is three miles south of M-72 on Herron Road.

22
Alba Had No Water

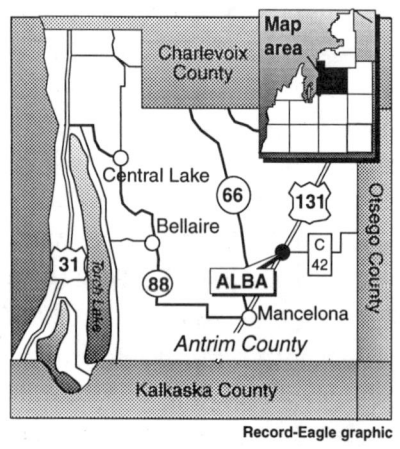
Record-Eagle graphic

In the beginning, the most serious problem facing the early settlers of Alba in Antrim County was lack of water. This seems strange, since the settlement was first called Cascade.

It was given that name by pioneer William J. Barker, who made the first clearing there in 1877 and platted the village in 1878. He was a Civil War veteran, and his business was real estate. He also kept a small store and was the first postmaster when the post office was opened in 1878. It was then that he renamed the village Alba which, as everyone knows, is Spanish for "white."

The Cascade is a small, swift stream that flows in a steep ravine to the Jordan River. But the closest it comes to Alba is two-and-one-half miles. So, lacking nearby open water, the early settlers had to look for other sources.

In the winter they melted snow. In spring they used the sap from maple trees and birches for cooking and washing clothes; the birch sap was best, because it was less sticky and because birches give twice as much sap as maples. In the summer, drinking water was brought up from Mancelona by hand car on the newly-arrived Grand Rapids and Indiana Railroad. But within a year or two, wells were driven—they had to go deep, ninety to one hundred feet—and the problem was solved. Or was it?

The first train arrived in 1877 and the railroad ended there until 1882, when the line was finished to Mackinac. To celebrate the event, some of the Alba people packed picnic lunches and rode hand cars to Mackinac.

Barker must have been a hot-shot real estate man because the village grew by leaps and bounds. In 1882, merchants Tom VanWert and L. M. Dibble platted an addition to the original plat. In just eighteen months the village had grown from 76 to over 500 residents.

Alba then had a handsome Methodist church, four grocery stores, a hotel and a boarding house (eventually it had three hotels), a drug store, a millinery shop,

The Detroit & Charlevoix Railroad crossed the Grand Rapids & Indiana Railroad at Alba in 1901. Painting by Jim Annis, entitled *East Jordan Bound.*

two broomhandle factories and a bowl factory, two sawmills, a newspaper (*The Record*), and various other shops and businesses. In 1901, Alba became a railroad junction when the Detroit and Charlevoix crossed the GR & I tracks on its way to Frederic.

Alba was on the move. Clearly it was destined for even greater things—a rural metropolis, to coin an oxymoron. Instead, it became a ghost town—"a little one-eyed, blinkin sort o' place," in Thomas Hardy's words. What happened? Why?

Perhaps one reason is its proximity to the much larger town of Mancelona, only six miles away. Another reason may have been its susceptibility to fire. In Alba hardly a year went by without something burn-

Right: The Congregational Church, Alba's first, was built in 1883 and was gutted by fire in 1993.

Below: The general store and home of Q. B. Stout was built a year after the big fire of 1893.

ing down. People say that until fairly recent times Alba never had enough water to control fires.

Here's a partial list of Alba fires:

1893—the Great Fire destroyed the entire business section of twenty-six buildings.

1897—the Alba Custom Mills—sawmill and gristmill—burned down.

1915—Anderson sawmill burned to the ground.

1916—Alba High School destroyed.

1948—Methodist Church burned down.

1993—Congregational Church, built in 1883, gutted by fire.

Among other Alba landmarks besides the Cascade are Deadman's Hill, where a young lumberjack was crushed by a runaway load of logs in 1910, and the Landslide, a precipice overlooking Cascade Creek, with a magnificent view of the Jordan River valley.

This happened on the way to The Landslide. We missed a turn and drove on a sandy two-track road past an old house trailer with a yard full of litter. Three minutes later we wound up at a dead end in a big open field bordered by woods on two sides. A hundred yards away, a man was puttering about, stooping now and then to examine something on the ground. The field around him was littered with small piles of trash.

I got out of the car and walked toward him, my shoes crunching on the dry spagnum moss. He saw me and stood waiting.

I said howdy when I was within speaking distance. He didn't reply.

In a louder voice, thinking he might be a little on the deaf side, I told him we were looking for The Landslide.

"How'd you get here?" he said. He was toothless, tanned and feisty-looking, wearing denims and a faded

Right: The Alba brick schoolhouse, built in 1881, is now an historical museum.

Left: The Eby boarding-house, one of Alba's oldest buildings, was built about 1890.

Right: DNR sign on Deadman's Hill.

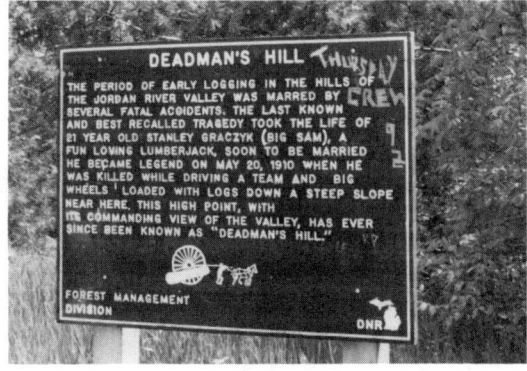

blue shirt. He looked about sixty, but could have been ten years younger or older. He had pale blue machine gunner's eyes.

I told him and said I hoped we weren't trespassing.

"This is my land," he said. "But that don't matter. You can't hurt nothing."

I asked him for directions to The Landslide.

"You missed a turn back there by my house," he said. "You should have stayed on the main road." Then he gave me detailed directions.

I asked him how far.

"Oh, it ain't far. Can't be more'n two, three miles." He paused, looking about. "How do you like my junkyard?"

Interesting, I said.

"I'm a man who hates to look at nothin'," he said. "You follow me?"

Not exactly.

"I let people dump their trash in here because otherwise there wouldn't be nothin' to look at. I need somethin' to look at. I hate looking at nothin'. Some people come in here a while ago and wanted to dump their trash in the woods over there. I told them not to dump in the woods where nobody can see it. I told them to dump it out here where people can see it. So they did."

That makes sense.

"You take some people, they ain't got nothing in their yard to look at, and you wonder what kind of people live there. Then you see a bunch of people on their front porch, drinkin' beer and having a lot of fun, and they's all kinds of things to look at in their yard. That's the kind of people I like."

I see your point.

"What do you think of that bunch in Lansing?" he asked, after a moment.

They've got their problems, haven't they.

"You ask me, all they're doin' is looking for a way to line their pockets."

So they say.

"You and me, we missed out," he said. "We should be workin' for the government. That's where the money is. Cradle to grave."

Right on, brother.

"You said it, brother."

I thanked him and went back to the car and turned around. He stood in the field watching as we drove away.

23
Meredith Revisited

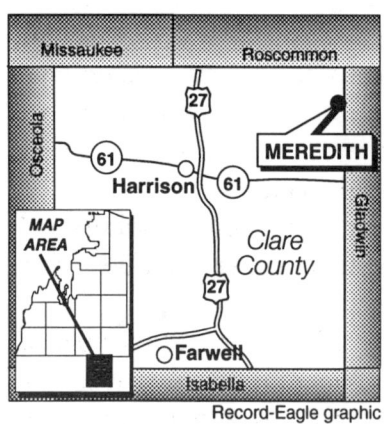
Record-Eagle graphic

Meredith had a short life but it cast a long shadow. A whole body of legend has grown up around it. Some of the stories are true or almost true; some have been greatly exaggerated; others are pure fantasy. Here are a few, all true or mostly true.

Jim Carr and his "wife" Maggie lured many girls into prostitution by running ads in metropolitan newspapers offering hotel work. The girls were met at the depot by a horse-drawn omnibus and taken to the "stockade," where they were stripped of their clothing, given a "wrap" and made virtual prisoners. Many were never seen or heard from again in the outside world. Some simply disappeared after their usefulness was over.

One exception was a girl named Jennie Kinney, who sought a position at Carr's in the winter of 1884-85. Somehow she managed to escape into the cold and to elude Carr's savage patrol dogs. She fled in her nightclothes through the snow to a house in town, where she was taken in by the woman owner.

An hour later, Carr and one of his goons knocked on the woman's door and demanded that she turn the girl over. "Wait here," she said, and disappeared into the house. After a few moments she returned with a loaded shotgun. "Begone, you rascals," she told them, "or I'll blow yez to kingdom come!"

Carr and his man departed without the girl and the woman was able to get her out of town on a train next day.

On December 1, 1884, Jim Carr sat in the bar of the Corrigan House in Meredith with two men—Sammy Johns and John Ryan, eager to make an easy buck. He offered them $250 if they'd help him burn down the rival "stockade" of Jim Silkworth at Arnold Lake, and they agreed. He told them to do it that night; meanwhile he'd take the train to Harrison and thus establish an alibi.

That night the two men walked the tracks to Arnold Lake, poured oil on the building, but were unable to light it, and fled when they thought they'd

The only gravestone that remains in the abandoned Meredith Cemetery. The marker reads:

> Edna
> Dau of
> St. & CA
> Ross
> Dec. 6, 1887

These fieldstones on the fringe of the Meredith Cemetery could mark the graves of Jim and Maggie Carr.

been detected. Carr, passing by on his return to Meredith three days later, saw that the building was still standing and was furious.

He met with Johns and Ryan at Meredith, and they agreed to have another go at it, with Carr personally directing the operation. Carr took the train to Arnold Lake, and the two men walked the tracks that night and met him at Silkworth's. Carr handed each of them a pistol and kept two for himself. He stood guard while Johns and Ryan placed shavings under the building, poured oil on them, and lit them with a match. They all retreated into the darkness as the kindling blazed and the building began to burn.

Soon the inmates came tumbling out of the house in their nightclothes and watched helplessly as the building went up in flames. Nobody was hurt, but Jim Silkworth's "stockade" burned to the ground.

Editor Foster of the *Gladwin Record* witnessed this scene on the train from Harrison to Meredith. Foster boarded the train and was followed by a well-built man with a pleasant face and manner, and wearing a black mustache, who sat down beside him.

A drunken lumberjack came up and accosted the stranger;

"Doing much business at Meredith?"

"None to mention," said the stranger.

"I wish you'd tell Jim Carr I want to see him."

"Do you know Jim Carr?"

"Yes, I'm well acquainted. I played violin for him in his bar for six months."

"Well, I'm Jim Carr," the stranger said. He got up and went into the smoking car, leaving the drunken lumberjack speechless.

It is said that after the death of Jim Carr and Maggie, 500 lumberjacks assembled in Meredith to give the pair a first-class funeral. However, none of the eight ministers they contacted would bury the wicked couple. So the lumberjacks chose one of their number—a big Swede, who was the only man who possessed a Bible—to conduct the services.

Jim and Maggie were too disreputable to be buried in the Meredith Cemetery. The graves lie somewhere just outside the abandoned cemetery and are marked only by fieldstones. Nobody knows the exact location.

Bill Beuche of Suttons Bay tells this story:

After his discharge from the Navy at the end of World War II, Bill got a job with Michigan Bell and spent three years in Osceola, Clare, and Gladwin counties mapping out rural telephone lines. During this time he became thoroughly familiar with the Meredith area and its folklore.

His work often took him along the Meredith Grade. The Grade was part of a logging railroad that the Flint and Pere Marquette built into the wilderness in 1881. It ran for ten miles from Frost Lake in Clare County to what is now Chaple Dam Road in Gladwin County passing through the town of Meredith, past Streaked Lake, and over the Cedar River. After the rails and ties had been taken up it became, without

The north branch of the Cedar River now flows through this culvert under the Meredith Grade.

The Meredith Grade 1993.

much improvement, a pretty fair auto road. Bill says he became so familiar with the sandy Grade that he used to drive it in the company Chevrolet coupe at 50 or 60 miles per hour.

He was traveling the Grade one day east of Meredith with his boss, the project engineer, a quiet man who answered to the name of Noah. Laconic was the word for Noah: he never used two words when one would do. He usually had a pipe clamped between his teeth and seldom removed it.

They were clipping along at around 50 mph when Noah unhurriedly took the pipe from his mouth and spoke for the first time in at least half an hour–just two words: "Bridge out."

"What?" said Bill absent-mindedly, wondering what the man was talking about.

Then, synapses flashing, he suddenly remembered: "The bridge! The Cedar River bridge!" and slammed on the brakes.

The car came to a slewing, shuddering stop at a 45-degree angle on the river bank, just short of the water.

And Noah, jammed up against the dashboard by the sudden stop, pipe still jutting angrily from his jaw, looked up and sideways at him in outraged astonishment, as if he were just now beginning to realize that he was at the mercy of a madman.

24
Colonville and Train Robber, John Smalley

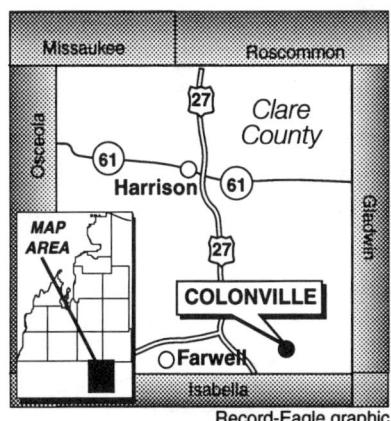
Record-Eagle graphic

In the perverse kind of way that people have of remembering the bad things that happen and not the good, Colonville is remembered chiefly because it was one of the hideouts of a notorious Michigan desperado. Most Michigan counties can't boast of even one desperado. Clare County had two—Jim Carr and John Smalley. Maybe that says something sinister about Clare County, but the people who live there don't think so. They think it just happened that way.

Colonville in Clare County should not be confused with Colon in St. Joseph County. Colon got its name when postmaster Lorensie Schellhouse opened a dictionary at random, saw the word 'colon,' and said: "We will call it Colon, for the river and the lake correspond exactly to the shape of a colon." This, needless to say, has spawned some rude jokes over the years.

How Colonville got its name is a mystery.

One of the first settlements in Clare County, it was originally called Bradley, after one of its pioneer settlers. But the first settler was David Smalley, who built a log cabin in 1870 on what is now called Athey Road. Civil War veteran Smalley became Sheridan Township's first supervisor. The first post office opened in 1894, with storekeeper Curtis Palmer as postmaster, and it operated until 1904.

David Smalley held other township offices and, as one of its most successful farmers, was held in high regard. He fathered a large family, and all the kids turned out well except one. The bad apple was John Smalley.

Smalley spent his early youth knocking about in the lumber camps along the Muskegon River. There he acquired a reputation as a very tough hombre—nobody in the camps dared tackle him, a friend said. Some time in the early 1880s, Smalley decided to change occupations. He and his gang robbed trains and banks for more than a decade, and he was so cool and clever at it that even though he never wore a disguise, the police didn't discover his identity until he died in a shoot-out in 1895.

The original Smalley family homestead log cabin on Athey Road. It has a new roof, the old one having been partly destroyed by fire.

Then in the prime of life at forty-one, he stood five feet eight inches tall, and weighed about 180 pounds. He had a full reddish beard and mustache. In the winter and summer he wore a dark sack overcoat with the side pockets removed so that he could draw his double-action pistols from his holster-belt with lightning speed. They called him "the whiskered train robber," a man of mystery. Heavily armed, extremely dangerous, approach with caution—that's how the "wanted" posters read. Whereabouts unknown.

Smalley and his gang were smart enough to operate a long way from home, sometimes as far as Oklahoma and Nebraska. After each heist, the gang would return to Michigan to scatter and lie low until the next

The log cabin interior.

job. Smalley's favorite hiding places were two vacant log cabins on Smalley family farms near Colonville.

Smalley's big mistake was robbing the Chicago and West Michigan passenger train on the night of August 20, 1895, at Fennville, Michigan. That was getting too close to home. The law traced Smalley to Grand Rapids, where he was challenged on a streetcar by a policeman named George Powers. Smalley killed the man with one point-blank shot to the face and made his escape cross-country to McBain. There he was ambushed the next night in a house belonging to his common-law wife Cora Brown, and died in a hailstorm of bullets from a posse of law officers. He lies now in an unmarked grave in the Mount View Cemetery at McBain.

Colonville today is just a crossroads. Nothing remains except a church and one of John Smalley's hideouts: the original one-story log cabin on Athey Road.

It has been completely restored and refurbished by the present owners of the property, the Herrick family, and is open to visitors. The family operates the Herrick Cheese Factory, a food and gift store, and is host also to several Amish shops; there's a large Amish colony in the Colonville area.

The other Smalley hideout, a two-story hewn log cabin, which stood on the Colonville Road, reportedly was torn down several years ago.

Amish horse-and-buggy on the Colonville road.

Note: A complete and detailed story of John Smalley's exploits is available in Larry Wakefield's book, *Butcher's Dozen: 13 Famous Michigan Murders.*

25
Leer and the Sinkholes

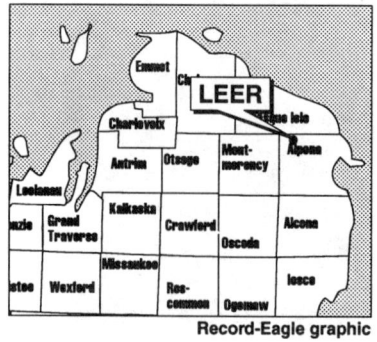
Record-Eagle graphic

Leer is a very satisfactory ghost town. It's the kind of lonely little village that might have inspired Thomas Gray to write his famous *Elegy written in a Churchyard*—one of Abraham Lincoln's favorite poems—if Gray had been an American living in northwest Alpena County in the twentieth century.

There never was much to the village itself in the way of business and population, but it has a picture-book church in the white, sparely elegant, pristine Colonial style, the only truly indigenous American architecture except for the skyscraper. The Leer

Lutheran Church was built in 1899, but the congregation itself recently celebrated their one-hundred-and-ten-year anniversary. The church has always been, and it still is, the social as well as the religious center of this community.

The churchyard is very satisfactory, too, and would have pleased Gray. It's full of nostalgia and gravestones bearing such names as Olsen, Christopherson, Heim and Alfsen, dating back to the 1880s. The earliest settlers were all Norwegian, and most of them were related. They came from a rural community in the Lier Valley a few miles west of Oslo.

The Leer Lutheran Church was built in 1899.

So it was natural that they should choose Leer (an Americanization of Lier) as the name for their post office, when it was granted in 1901. John Carl Alfsen became its first postmaster, and the office operated until 1935.

These young Norwegians came to America for one purpose: they wanted to farm their own land. This wasn't possible in Norway, where only three percent of the land is arable and almost all of it was owned by wealthy landlords. There, a young man wanting to farm had only two options. He could spend the rest of his life working for the landlord, or he could emigrate. Some of the best, brightest and boldest chose the latter course.

The number of Norwegian immigrants to this country in the nineteenth century was second only to the Irish. The young men from Lier, some married but mostly single, chose Alpena because work was available at the Fletcher Lumber Company in the lumber camps in winter and in the sawmills in summer. Over time they could save enough money to buy farmland. But they had no intention of settling there permanently. Alpena's fifty-two saloons made the place somewhat less than suitable for raising a family.

The first settlers at Leer were Andreas Christopherson, Otter Olsen, Gustav Gullicksen, and Bernhard Enger, who built the first log cabin. Others soon followed. They chose the area because the rolling green hills and forests reminded them of home. Immigrants were willing to leave their homeland for better

This candy and ice cream store was built around 1900 by Olaf Alfsen. It's the only remaining business building in Leer.

opportunities in a strange new land, but they wanted the new land to look and feel as much like home as possible.

They bought land from the Fletcher Lumber Company, which had logged the pine timber and was eager to sell it cheap. Their biggest problem in clearing it was getting rid of the big pine stumps, many of which were three, four and even five feet in diameter, and in some places so close together that kids could travel a considerable distance by jumping from one to another without ever touching the ground. (Hence the word "stump-jumper.")

First they tried to dig them out, but that was too slow. Next they used stump-pullers, powered by horses, and managed to get out two or three a day, which they used for fencing. Then somebody suggested dynamite, but at first they were too cautious and didn't use

This abandoned house near Leer was built by the Lumsden family more than 100 years ago.

The Michael Elowski grist mill on the Thunder Bay River near Lee was built around 1890.

enough. Finally, one of the boldest, Otter Olsen, used eight sticks on one stump and blew it all over his forty acres.

Gunhild Christopherson had a stump problem, too, but more particularly with her husband. She wanted to plant a flower garden just outside their cabin window, but the space she chose was occupied by a huge pine stump. Andreas said he had more important things to do than pulling up stumps for flowers. So, when he left for Alpena one day to buy supplies, Gunhild herself attacked the stump with an axe, and when her husband returned the next day he was astonished to find that the stump had been replaced by a flower garden.

The first public building in Leer was the school, which was built in 1882 and was used also for church services until the church itself was completed in 1899. By 1900, Leer had a sawmill and gristmill, two general stores, a blacksmith shop and a lime kiln, and a church membership of over 100—but no saloon. By 1925 there were more than fifty families there.

And then there are the sinkholes. The sinkholes are a geographic and geological phenomenon especially prevalent in the Leer area and in south-central Presque Isle County, just across the line. They were formed when ground water scoured out subterranean caverns in the porous Devonian limestone that underlies most of northeastern lower Michigan—and then the roof fell in. The overburden of earth and rock gave way and exposed roughly cylindrical holes some 200 feet deep and several hundred feet across.

In a southeastern mile-long line just east of Leer are six sinkholes, all of about the same width and depth, indicating that they were formed by the same underground stream. Their perpendicular sides suggest that they are of comparatively recent origin,

"Mystery Valley"

The sinkhole at the corner of Leer Road and Maple Valley Road.

possibly within the last hundred years. Others in the area, with eroded sides, are older. At "Mystery Valley," a mile-and-a-half north of Leer, a surface stream sinks underground and leaves its valley curiously dry.

The Leer area is full of sinkholes of various sizes. Some, the natives say, are in the making, and they half expect to wake up some morning and find one of them in the back forty or even in the front yard—though they aren't losing any sleep over it. Most of the sinkholes are on private land, but one on the corner of Leer Road and Maple Valley Road, a mile south of the Norwegian Church, is easily accessible to visitors.

But if you suffer from vertigo, don't get too near the edge. The drop is 200 feet, straight down.

26
Antrim City Died Aborning

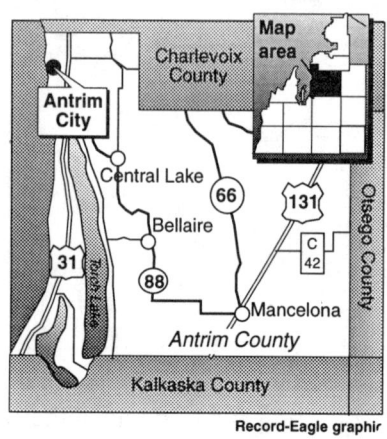

Record-Eagle graphic

Antrim City in northwestern Antrim County had high hopes. The city fathers named the village a city because they fully expected it to become one. But it never really had a chance and even as a village it had one of the shortest lives of any ghost town in Michigan.

The first settler was Richard D. Orr, who built a house and barn on the north side of Antrim Creek in

1859 or '60. Later, with a partner named Walderon, he built and operated a small sawmill. He also became Antrim City's first postmaster on July 21, 1862.

But the real city fathers were two farm boys from Clinton County, New York, brothers Lucius H. and John W. Pearl, and a man named Orvis Wood. Together, in 1861 or thereabouts, they launched a shipping business at Antrim City. At a cost of some $6,000 (a lot of money in those days) they built a long dock and began shipping logs, lumber, shingles, railroad ties, and fence posts to markets in Milwaukee and Chicago.

The trouble was that the dock wasn't long enough—nor was the second one they built a few years later. Antrim City had no natural harbor, and the water offshore was so shallow that the larger boats had to anchor a considerable distance offshore. The goods they brought to Antrim City had to be lightered to the dock in smaller craft, while the cargo of logs and lumber had to be rafted out and hauled aboard the boats: an inefficient and laborious process.

Only such smaller boats as Traverse City's *Sunny Side* were able to tie up at the dock. *Sunny Side*, a small steamer, was purchased by the Hannah Lay Lumber Company in 1864 for service around Grand Traverse Bay. She began regular trips under Captain Joe Emory in the spring of 1865. Departing Traverse City at seven a.m., she called at Elk Rapids, Antrim City, Pine River (Charlevoix), Old Mission, Bowers Harbor, and Suttons Bay, returning to her Traverse City berth every evening.

The Rex Beach house.

In 1866, she got a new captain, John Drake, and spacious new upper-deck cabins. But on November 22 of the following year she was storm-driven against the dock at Charlevoix and dashed to pieces. Incidentally, the *Sunny Side* is the boat whose whistle figures prominently in a charming children's book, *Whistle Up the Bay* by Nancy Stone. It was illustrated by Atwood resident Betty Beebe, a member of the pioneer Pearl family.

In 1867, Orvis Wood and Lucius Pearl realized their mistake, moved their operation a few miles north, started the village of Norwood, and built a dock there. As a harbor, Norwood wasn't much better than Antrim City, but the water was deeper offshore and the big boats were able to load and unload at the dock. Norwood lasted as long as the hardwood lumber held out, and then the Pearls returned to something they were good at, which was farming.

Antrim City lingered a few years after the Pearls departed. In 1867, the sawmill was still running and Dexter & Noble of Elk Rapids had just opened a new branch store there with J. N. Sickles as manager. Orvis Wood was still shipping wood products at the dock, and Wait & Wood had just finished a new general store and were fixing to start a potash company. By 1884, however, almost nothing was left of the village.

Antrim City's one slender claim to distinction is that it was the boyhood home of writer Rex Beach, who in 1871 was born on a farm on what is now called Rex Beach Road. Beach was the author of many popular outdoor novels in the vein of Jack London and Jim Hendryx.

And if you like cemeteries, don't miss the one at Antrim City, on Dixie Highway just south of the old school: it and the school are all that's left of the village.

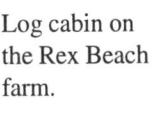
Log cabin on the Rex Beach farm.

The cemetery lies on a hill above the lakeshore, and the graves, many of them dating back to the 1870s, are shaded by giant maple and beech trees well over a hundred years old. People come from miles around to sit in their shade and muse about those pioneers of bygone days.

Antrim City Cemetery.

27
Levi Lupton Was a Rascal But He Built a Town

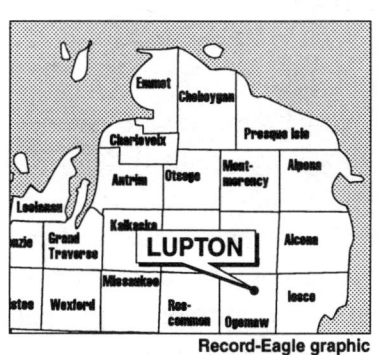
Record-Eagle graphic

Michigan bad guys generally came in three categories in descending order of wickedness: scoundrel, desperado, and rascal. Jim Carr of Meredith was a scoundrel. John Smalley of Colonville was a desperado. Levi Lupton of Lupton was a rascal. What made him an interesting rascal was that he was also a widely-travelled evangelist and the most popular preacher in the Lupton Friends Church.

The ghost town of Lupton at the headwaters of the Rifle River in Ogema County was originally called

Levi R. Lupton   Courtesy of Phebe Cotton.

Lane Heights. It was first settled in 1879 by Quakers from Ohio and Indiana. Among them were Emmor Lupton (for whom the village was named), his wife Rebecca, three sons and three daughters, Levi, Isaac, Martin, Eva, Sarah, and Lucina. Other early settlers were the Rakestraws, Holes, Dobsons and Hamiltons. Lane Heights stood about a mile north of the present village site. It was given a post office as Lane on April 11, 1881: Levi Lupton was its first postmaster.

The Luptons took title to about 300 acres and cleared 125 acres. In 1889, they built a sawmill and shingle mill on Levi's farm. It had a capacity of 25,000 feet of lumber and 20,000 shingles per day. The lumber and shingles were hauled by wagon to the Maltby switch of the Detroit Bay City & Alpena's Loon Lake branch, nine miles east in Iosco County.

Meanwhile, the Luptons had been working hard for years to persuade the railroad to build a branch into Ogema County and a spur to the sawmill. Their efforts were finally rewarded on January 1, 1893, when the first train arrived. Following the flat land it missed Lane Heights by a mile or so, but that didn't worry Levi Lupton. He had already anticipated that and made provisions for it.

Levi R. Lupton, a good-looking young man with soulful brown eyes and enormous energy—especially popular with the ladies—was thinking big. A year or two earlier, he had conceived a grand scheme for building a new town near the railroad. With several partners he formed a land syndicate, sold debentures, and by the time the railroad arrived, the new town was already under construction, with a depot and several other buildings completed. The Quaker church on Lane Heights was dismantled in 1892 and rebuilt on a

Lupton in 1893 when the railroad arrived. Courtesy of Phebe Cotton.

View of Lane Heights. Courtesy of Phebe Cotton.

new town site. In 1893, the new town and its post office were renamed Lupton; Joshua Rakestraw was the new postmaster.

The new town covered 147 acres. Its streets were already laid out and named; some even had board sidewalks. The main street, Ogema Avenue, was over a mile long and wide enough to accommodate a planned trolley car. Industrial sites had been marked out and provided with railroad access. Shade trees were planted and a town park planned. No expense was spared in the plan to make Lupton the most modern and progressive town in northern Michigan.

Levi's plans were visionary. He spelled them out in a 32-page, illustrated booklet entitled *One Year of Lupton, Pioneer Day, July 4, 1893*; it was designed to attract new business, industry and residents to the town. They included a three-story 35-room hotel with

Sketch of the big hotel in the promotional booklet; it was never built. Courtesy of Phebe Cotton.

This building, built in 1899, was probably Reid's hardware store.

The Quaker Church and the school on Lane Heights. The church, built in 1889, was moved to Lupton in 1892. Courtesy of Phebe Cotton.

the latest amenities and "a table second to none in northern Michigan"; also a three-story office building, a townhall, and other institutions.

Above all, Lupton would be a temperance town. Liquor traffic would be forbidden. Each deed had a provision or conveyance that no liquor would ever be served on the premises.

Lupton grew during the next ten years but fell short of what its founder had envisioned. Leander Hole had a general store. Jim Hamilton built a small hotel and blacksmith shop. Alex Reid had a grocery store and a hardware store. The Drexel house next to the hotel housed the Lupton Land Syndicate offices. In addition, the town had sawmills, livery stables, a meat market, millinery shop, shoemaker's shop, lumber and real estate offices, drugstore, and meat market—and a population of 100 in 1905. A new brick school was built in 1903.

And that was it: no big hotel or office buildings, no new factories, no trolley car. And when it came time to settle the accounts, it was found that the Lupton Land Company was bankrupt. The people who had invested money in the scheme—and they included most of the villagers—felt they had been swindled.

Yet, to the town's great surprise, Levi Lupton continued to go about his business as if nothing had happened, enduring black looks and muttered insults with an equanimity that astonished them. Eventually, however, he moved to Alliance, Ohio, where he started a Bible school.

And later, when word came back that he was in trouble again—this time with a young lady—his enemies said, well, they weren't surprised, but were

The Lupton school was built in 1903; now in use as a senior citizens center.

sorry for his poor wife, Laura, whom everybody loved and regarded as a saint. And even some of the few people who still believed in him had to admit that perhaps his character was flawed.

Was Levi Lupton a swindler or just a visionary who over-reached himself? The debate continues to this day. The Lupton schoolmaster, Lawrence Dunlap (who lost money but was able, over Levi's protests, to take most of it out in trade) called him a swindler. Dunlap kept a diary from 1890 to 1919. In an entry dated December 27, 1896, he described Levi Lupton's flamboyant preaching style:

"Levi preached and overturned the table and chair in imitation of the money changers."

In another, much later, he wrote the perfect epitaph for the failed Lupton enterprise, quoting *Nehemiah 7-4*: "Now the city was large and great; but the people were few therein, and the houses were not builded."

This is all that's left of Lupton's "downtown" today.

29
Comins: End of the Line

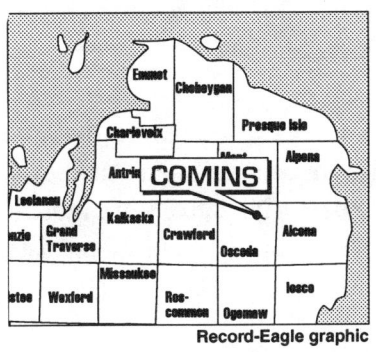
Record-Eagle graphic

Comins is probably the only ghost town in Michigan that cheerfully admits it's a ghost town—not only admits but actually advertises it. A roadside sign at the village limits says, "WELCOME TO COMINS: The Ghost Town with a Lot of Spirit." It was put there by a real estate company with offices in Comins and West Branch.

About one hundred people still live in Comins, and they are mostly elderly because the young people had to look elsewhere for jobs—jobs are scarce in Comins. In addition to the realty company there are maybe half a dozen small businesses, including a

The interior of the H. M. Loud Company general store at Comins, around 1900. Courtesy of the Steiner Museum Collection.

saloon and a hotel. The hotel has an interesting history. It no longer offers overnight accommodations, but it still serves three meals a day. The patrons are mostly local people, with an occasional carload of tourists who either are taking a short cut to Lewiston on the back roads or have lost their way.

The hotel dining room seats about twenty-five people, but on a typical day maybe only a dozen will drop in for lunch: farmers, truck drivers, carpenters, and a group of "ladies of the club" engaged in animated conversation and having a lot of fun. Now and then a man will sit down with them for a few minutes of light-hearted repartee. The food's good, and the prices are modest. The wing dings and fries are especially tasty.

The Carrie James Hotel was once a boarding house in Lewiston. Originally it was called the Cleve-

Comins in 1905. The depot at center; Loud general store left rear; Rust boarding house right center; Solomon store right rear. Courtesy of the Steiner Museum Collection.

The Carrie James Hotel.

land Hotel. That's because Clarence "Hooky" Cleveland bought the place in 1919, dismantled it and rebuilt it in Comins piece by piece. He and his wife ran the hotel until 1929, when they sold it to John and Carrie James of Houghton Lake, who in later years sold it to somebody else. Cleveland was called "Hooky" be-

The Knothole Bar.

cause he had lost one of his hands in a sawmill accident and wore an artificial iron one (not a hook) in its place. Apparently "Hooky" didn't resent his insensitive nickname.

During Prohibition "Hooky" was arrested for moonshining and did a short stretch in the Big House. He said afterwards that he was glad that the law caught up with him when it did because he was able to learn so much in the penal institution. He said he profited from the experience.

Comins (pronounced "come ins") is five miles north of Fairview (which calls itself the "turkey capitol" of Michigan) in northern Oscoda County. It was the offspring of the H. M. Loud Lumber Company of Oscoda and the AuSable and Northwestern logging railroad. After the Louds finished logging off the timber in the AuSable River valley, they moved their headquarters north from McKinley and started the village of Comins, which they named for one of the earliest settlers, Coolidge H. Comins. The Louds built a big general store in Comins about 1900, and moved their lumberman's library and reading room up from McKinley to serve as the village's first depot. The railroad ended there as far as passengers were concerned, and Comins was therefore called "the end of the line." The depot building still stands; it is now in use as a residence.

The timber lasted about ten years. The Louds then began running advertisements in midwestern newspa-

Now a residence, this building was the lumberman's library and reading room at McKinley. It was moved to Comins to serve as the first depot on the AuSable & Northwestern Railroad.

During Prohibition hard liquor was dispensed in this log cabin near the Knothole Bar.

pers offering the cutover land at bargain prices. Their best customers were Mennonite and Amish families from Ohio and Indiana; and their descendents comprise much of the area's population today. They are a friendly, hard-working and happy people—but don't ask the Amish to pose for snapshots. It's against their religion. Their strict religious beliefs forbid them to have anything to do with graven images.

The village itself prospered for a while. About 1916, the railroad was taken over by the Detroit and Mackinac Railroad and widened to standard gauge. By that time Comins had two general stores, a hotel and boarding house, a blacksmith shop, a grist mill, and a saloon. Decline set in when the D & W abandoned the Comins branch in 1927.

The only business in Comins never to go out of business is the Knothole Bar. It was started in the early 1900s by Frank and Reva Pfaff, and it's still going strong. During Prohibition they served near beer and soft drinks at the bar; the hard stuff was dispensed to carefully selected customers in a little log cabin nearby.

No trip to Comins is complete (as they say) without a visit to "Boiling Springs." In a small forest pond about half the size of a tennis court, several springs boil up from limestone depths, churning the sand. These steadily flowing waters are the source of Gilchrist Creek, which flows north into the Thunder Bay River, which empties into Lake Huron at Alpena.

The springs are on private land—a vast tract of wilderness owned by a downstate sportsmen's club, where Howard Shelley of *Michigan Outdoors* fame has a summer home and Mort Neff himself spent a lot of time fishing and hunting. Permission to visit the springs and directions to it are available at the clubhouse on request.

"Boiling Springs" near Comins.

29
Essex Disappeared

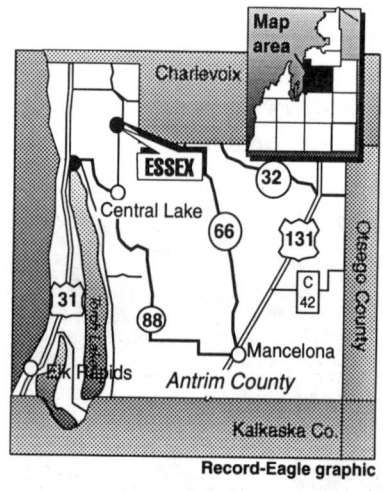

Unlike America's Far West, where the dry climate has kept old mining towns virtually intact, Michigan's weather is hard on abandoned buildings. Even so, most Michigan ghost towns have managed to leave at least something behind to mark the spot—an empty house or barn, a ruined foundation wall; even, in some cases, a cluster of abandoned store fronts.

Yet there are some where nothing at all remains except memories, which to paraphrase Joseph Conrad, every year grow dim, grow cold, grow small, and expire.

Mention Essex even to a Michigan history buff, and all you're likely to get is a blank stare. That's because hardly anyone outside the vicinity has ever heard of it, let alone knows where it is. It doesn't appear on any current map; it isn't even on Essex Road. Without somebody to give you directions, you'd have a hard time finding it.

Essex lies in Banks Township in the northeast corner of Antrim County near Ellsworth. If you drive a quarter of a mile south of Essex Road on Dennis Road, you will come to a little valley where a small creek passes under the road. It's called King Creek, and it's easy to miss in the tall grass. But it was here in

The big steam-powered sawmill at Essex, 1899.

161

The boarding house at Essex was owned by Joseph Dennis, who stands dressed in a suit in front of the doorway. Note the cook with his long bullhorn which called the men to meals. Courtesy of Banks Township Historical Society.

this peaceful valley, almost a hundred years ago, that the sawmill town of Essex was home to at least 200 people—some say as many as 400.

Essex was born in 1899 when the Central Lake Lumber Company built a spur of the Pere Marquette Railroad into the valley from Dix, a former stop on the main line a few miles below Ellsworth. They dammed King Creek for a pond to wash the logs in, and began to cut the pine, hardwood and hemlock in the area. Most of the mill hands were Hollanders from Grand Rapids, who responded to the company's ad in the city newspaper for fifty men and ten teams of horses.

The big sawmill and the logpiles and lumber completely filled the narrow valley. The workers built their houses in the hills on both sides, and the whine of the big mill saw became a part of their lives, day and night. By 1903, Essex had a big general store (run by the Vandenberg brothers), a boarding house, blacksmith shop, shoe shop ("Shoes Repard Hear"), livery stable, telephone office, and post office; it opened on November 13, 1900 and operated until 1904. Henry Chamberlin was the first postmaster.

Eventually, Essex also had two sawmills, a shingle mill, and a stave factory. The Dutchmen were frugal, hard-working, and sober, and the town never had a saloon, though whiskey was available not far away for those who indulged.

The first school was built over one of the horse barns. Classes were held there until the teacher and kids couldn't stand the barnyard smell any longer. Somebody donated land on the hill to the north, and a

Lumber camp near Essex. Courtesy of Banks Township Historical Society.

proper school was built. Its concrete front steps still remain in an open field where the school once stood, a lone remnant of the town.

Many people once lived at Essex, and they did most of the things that people do. But the one event that everybody remembered was a tragi-comedy. A young lumberjack was killed while clowning on a pile of logs. His name was Harry Bradford and it happened on January 29, 1902.

He was showing off, the villagers said, in a demonstration of his agility by bounding up and down and dancing around on a skid of big logs. The pile loosened up and the logs began to roll, and instead of doing the sensible thing by jumping off to one side or the other, he tried to climb the moving pile. Result: the logs rolled over him, and that was the last of Harry Bradford.

His death was "immortalized" in a poem by a local rhymester. Of its twenty or more stanzas, this one will have to suffice:

> *It was on the twenty-ninth of January in 1902,*
> *Little did we think there would be one life lost*
> *in our brave lumbering crew;*
> *Little did we think there in the morning*
> *That before the close of day*
> *That our noble friend would be doomed to go*
> *To his cold silent grave.*

Bradford's cold silent grave is in Ellsworth Cemetery. Essex didn't last long enough to have one of its own.

30
Shelldrake and Irishman Con Culhane

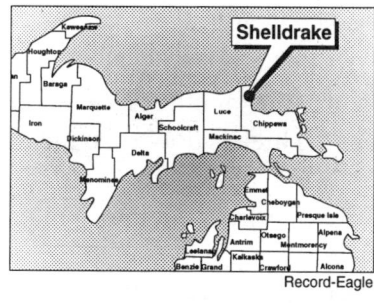

The time: October 1879. The place: Whitefish Bay in Lake Superior.

Perhaps without even knowing it, the crew of the tugboat *Grace* is embarked on a perilous mission. Since 1870 *Grace* has ferried freight and passengers between the two Saults, Canada, and America. On this trip, however, she is engaged in towing a scow with a piledriver to Goulais Bay on the Canadian side, where a dock is to be built.

What makes the mission perilous is that October is one of the two worst months for storms on Lake Superior, known as the "graveyard of ships."

View of Main Street in Shelldrake 1900. Post office third from left. Courtesy of Julie Wilber.

All goes well until early in the evening, when they are well past Iroquois Point at the mouth of Whitefish Bay. Then the tugboat engine breaks down. To make matters worse, a strong wind blows up from the southeast. Out of control, *Grace* drifts out into Whitefish Bay.

During the night, the wind reaches gale force. In an effort to save the ferry boat, the Captain orders the crew to cut a scow adrift, and they part the towlines with an axe.

In the fury of the storm *Grace* is driven onto a sandbar about 200 feet offshore from Shelldrake. She soon fills with water and is pounded to pieces. But the crew makes it safely ashore in the shallow water.

Upon reaching the shore the Captain climbs up the bank and with the crew gathered round he praises God for their deliverance.

"Thank God!" he says, "We are all safe!"

Then he drops dead with a heart attack.

Because no one is living at Shelldrake at that time, his body is taken by boat to Whitefish Point. Later the scow is found high and dry on the beach and is returned to the Sault.

The ghost town of Shelldrake lies in northern Chippewa County on Whitefish Bay between Paradise and Whitefish Point. Originally known as Edwards (after an early settler) it came into being in 1895, when the Moore, Parke & Sharpe Lumber Company built a sawmill there and began logging the Tahquamenon River watershed. Along with the mill, the company built a model village. It was built on both sides of the main street that extended for almost half a mile along the shore of Whitefish Bay. There were houses for the

This house, now privately owned, is said to have been the home of the company manager, a man named Bartlett. An uncle of the present owner won the house in a poker game many years ago. Courtesy of Julie Wilber.

millhands and their families, a hotel, general store, hospital and school, and an icehouse that could store enough meat to feed as many as 1,000 people during the winter months when the town was virtually isolated. The hotel was named Ishkabibble Inn by a Jewish peddler after a famous Jewish comedian.

A boardwalk ran the full length of the town. All the buildings had plastered walls and were piped for hot water and heat from the sawdust burner at the mill. The company also built a big dock into the bay, with a tramway for carrying lumber from the mill to be loaded on steamers for shipment down the lakes.

The village was named for a duck. Shelldrake is a merganser fish-eating duck that was plentiful on Whitefish Bay and the Shelldrake River. The village was awarded a post office in 1905, with George N. Hutton as the first postmaster. Mail was brought by stage-

Shelldrake today. The building at right was the post office.

Con Culhane

coach in the summer and by dogsled in winter from Eckerman, twenty-some miles south.

A logging railroad brought logs to the mill from twelve lumbercamps in the area. The logging contractor was Con Culhane, a figure of almost mythic Paul Bunyan proportions in Michigan logging history. The story goes that he got into the lumbering business because his wife Ellen told him he was too smart to be pulling stumps on their small farm near Bay City.

Culhane first began logging in 1893 in the Big Two Hearted River area, and he built his first logging railroad there. In 1895 he contracted with Moore, Parke & Sharpe to supply their mill at Shelldrake. Con boasted later that he never owned a stick of pine timber, but had made a fortune logging for other people.

Con was a man of tremendous strength and agility. He loved logging, railroading, practical joking, and fighting—but most of all he loved Ellen, whom he called "my pretty woman." She was the driving force in his life.

By "fighting" he meant "wrestling"—though he could use his fists too if the situation warranted. It was said that he tried his strength against every man who came to him for a job, sometimes with Ellen holding a lantern while the two men grappled outdoors on a frosty evening. "Any man who can fight can work" was his motto. Others were turned away. Despite low pay and long hours his men idolized him.

He died as he had lived, with his boots on. He was killed on his own logging train near Shelldrake. From his seat on the engine tender he went back over the flatcars to talk to his brakeman. The train gave a violent lurch as he was crossing from one car to another and threw him under the wheels. He died instantly.

In 1899, the copper mining company, Calumet & Hecla, bought the mill and uncut timber, continuing the contract with Con Culhane for railroading the logs, though his bid was higher than several others. They shipped large quantities of timbers for their mines.

Around 1910, Calumet & Helca sold out to Bartlett Brothers, a Canadian firm. Because the Bartlett operation seemed plagued by accidents, some of its employees thought it was "jinxed." Several men were killed in accidents, and the mill burned down in 1910. It was replaced by a mill brought up from Deward, Michigan,

Michigan Historic Site marker at Shelldrake.

where the last timber holdings of Michigan lumber king David Ward were harvested from 1900 to 1910. But that mill, too, burned down in 1925, and that was the end of Shelldrake.

In 1979, a former Detroit businessman, Brent Biehl, bought 300 acres including most of the townsite of Shelldrake and five of its original buildings. He plans to restore it as an historical village, open to tourists, but the work has gone slowly because he has also been establishing a plant for making barbecue fire briquets out of hardwood sawdust and woodchips.

31
Whitefish Point: Cranberries, Whitefish, Shipwrecks

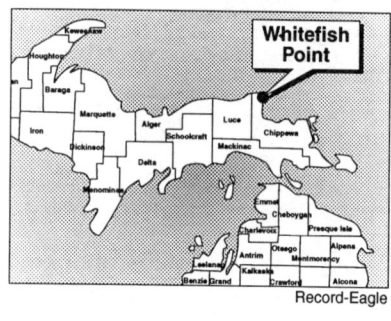
Record-Eagle

Whitefish Point in northwestern Chippewa County is one of the oldest ghost towns in Michigan. It was an Indian settlement long before white men came. The first Indian camp meeting took place there in July of 1852. More than 200 Indians attended. They came from all over the north country: from Keweenaw Bay, Garden River and Manitoulin Island, as well as the Tahquamenon and Naomikong areas.

The Whitefish Point light is the oldest active light on Lake Superior.

The meeting was conducted by an Indian preacher named Jones and three white missionaries, who were given Indian names. They had good weather and plenty of food. The Whitefish Bay Indians supplied whitefish, and the missionaries provided bread and other food.

Thirty Indians were converted to Christianity, and one marriage was solemnized. One hundred fifteen Indians took the pledge of total abstinence. A collection of $40 was taken; one widow gave all she had— 40 cents.

Three years earlier, the first lighthouse—a brick tower—was established at Whitefish Point. The present tower and a coastguard station were built around 1900.

The Coast Guard Station at Whitefish Point was built around 1900; it is no longer in operation.

The light, foghorn, and radio beacon were automated in 1971 and are controlled from Sault Ste. Marie. Whitefish Point light is the oldest active light on Lake Superior.

The first white settlers arrived in the early 1870s when Whitefish Point became a supply landing for the lumbercamps in the area. It had already become a commercial fishery for the export of fresh and salted whitefish. A post office was awarded in 1877; Sylvester P. Mason was its first postmaster. In 1879, the population was 59.

The village languished for a while after most of the timber was gone, but got its second wind in the late 1880s, when the fishery was expanded and a new cash crop was established—cranberries. By 1900 there were a dozen cranberry growers in the area, and the village reached a peak population of 200 in 1905.

John Clarke and Alex Barclay, a retired sea captain, had started raising cranberries in the area as early as 1872. Clarke cultivated wild vines and established them in large marshes known as bogs. By the use of sluice-gates he controlled the water level, and when the cranberries were ripe he flooded the bogs, and the berries were harvested using rakes and steel tines. The berries floated and were scooped up in wire-mesh scoops. The work was done by Indians, who pitched their teepees between the bogs and the beach.

The berries were washed, dried and sorted, and packed in wooden bushel crates. They were then taken to Booth's dock at Whitefish Point and shipped by steamer to fruit merchants in Chicago, Buffalo and

Whitefish Point is known as the graveyard of Lake Superior.

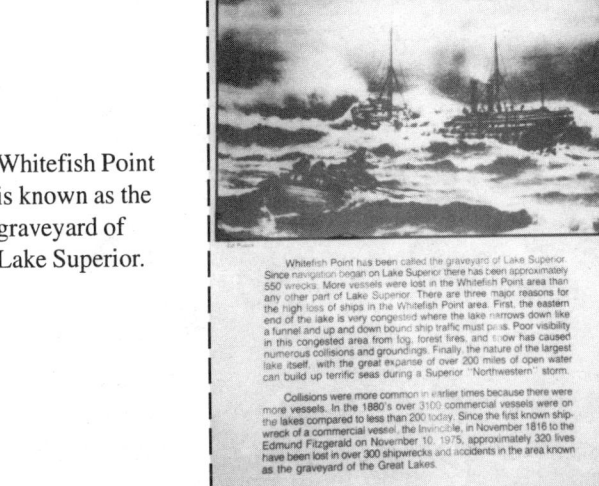

Graveyard of the Great Lakes

Whitefish Point has been called the graveyard of Lake Superior. Since navigation began on Lake Superior there has been approximately 550 wrecks. More vessels were lost in the Whitefish Point area than any other part of Lake Superior. There are three major reasons for the high loss of ships in the Whitefish Point area. First, the eastern end of the lake is very congested where the lake narrows down like a funnel and up and down bound ship traffic must pass. Poor visibility in this congested area from fog, forest fires, and snow has caused numerous collisions and groundings. Finally, the nature of the largest lake itself, with the great expanse of over 200 miles of open water can build up terrific seas during a Superior "Northwestern" storm.

Collisions were more common in earlier times because there were more vessels. In the 1880's over 3100 commercial vessels were on the lakes compared to less than 200 today. Since the first known shipwreck of a commercial vessel, the Invincible, in November 1816 to the Edmund Fitzgerald on November 10, 1975, approximately 320 lives have been lost in over 300 shipwrecks and accidents in the area known as the graveyard of the Great Lakes.

Detroit. Clarke raised several hundred bushels annually. He also sold cranberry catsup and jelly. Cranberry growers in other parts of Michigan came to him for advice.

Frank House took over the Whitefish Point cranberry establishment from John Clarke. He raised berries until his death in 1935. After that, the crops were small. Without constant care the bogs grew up in tag alder, marsh grass, and moss, the enemies of cranberry growers. Yet even as late 1975 Bert Hutton, Frank House's son-in-law, single-handedly picked ninety-four bushels of berries from the bogs on the House cranberry farm.

The final blow came in 1975 with a big storm that sank the *Edmund Fitzgerald*. It changed the sand dunes along the lake at the mouth of the creek that drained the bogs. This raised the water level in the bogs and resulted in moss growth that choked out the cranberry vines.

The Shipwreck Museum at Whitefish Point.

The whitefish fishery had long since given up the ghost.

Whitefish Point has an excellent maritime museum and gift shop and is now a magnet for tourists. The lighthouse, its gleaming white tower rising as gracefully as a Greek temple, still guides the big boats in and out of Whitefish Bay. But, except for one or two crumbling old wooden buildings, nothing remains of the village itself.

32
Thompsonville: The Biggest Little Town in Michigan

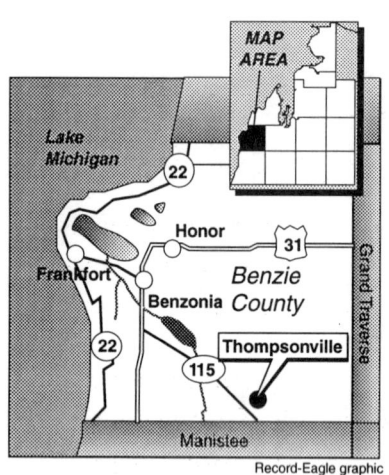

Record-Eagle graphic

In 1901, the village of Thompsonville in Benzie County was pushing out its chest and flexing its muscles and calling itself the "Biggest Little Town in Michigan." That was the title of a promotional booklet put out by the Thompsonville Improvement Association (the equivalent of today's chamber of commerce) for distribution downstate.

Diamond House Hotel, one of the finest in northern Michigan, was built about 1895 by Ella Diamond, a widow from St. Charles, Michigan. It burnt down in 1902, was rebuilt and did business until 1928 when it was again destroyed by fire. Courtesy of Thompsonville Historical Society.

Some of this boasting was typical booster bombast, of course, designed to lure more settlers to the backwoods community. But a lot of it was genuine. The people of Thompsonville really believed that their town was destined to become the metropolis of the north.

And why not? In the ten years since its birth, the town had grown to 1,200 people. Forty-eight shops lined both sides of Main Street. The town also had two hotels, three saloons, a bakery, two churches, a weekly newspaper, and a four-room schoolhouse with an enrollment of 300 pupils. It also had two sawmills, a cooperage factory, charcoal kilns for the production of

Junction of Pere Marquette and Ann Arbor railroads at Thompsonville around 1900, showing both railroad depots.

pig iron, a chemical plant, a planing mill, a handle factory, three blacksmiths and carriage shops, a bank, and a cigar factory.

The town was founded in 1890 by the half-dozen heirs of Sumner S. Thompson of Massachusetts and the Reverend Henry Ward Beecher of Brooklyn. (Beecher is remembered as a champion of abolition and women's rights—and for his trial in 1874 in a suit for damages by Theodore Tilton, who charged that Beecher had committed adultery with his wife. The trial ended in a hung jury, leaving Beecher's reputation somewhat tarnished). Before the town was incorporated as Thompsonville in 1893, the southwest end was known as Beecher.

Thompsonville was strategically situated at a junction of the Pere Marquette and Ann Arbor railroads—121 miles north of Grand Rapids, twenty-seven miles southwest of Traverse City, and twenty-three miles southeast of Frankfort. The promotional booklet called it "the most pleasant and most favored spot for a prosperous town in all the great expanse of Michigan's great peninsula."

That was an exaggeration, of course, but the area did have considerable assets in natural beauty and resources. The hills were covered with rich stands of hardwoods, and good crops of hay, oats, and corn could be raised in the valleys between. Along the Betsey River bottom, the soil was rich enough for potatoes and garden produce.

A Professor Borradaile of the Agricultural College at Lansing, took samples of the soil and reported that it contained generous amounts of nitrogen and lime. "I see no reason," the Professor opined, "why, under proper tillage, your country should not be one of the most productive in the state."

In addition, there were outcroppings of red hematite (iron ore) within a mile or two of the village, and

Thompsonville's main street, once lined by forty-eight business and shop buildings, is almost deserted today.

This was Thompsonville's grist mill, electrically operated. The story is that it was moved here from Copemish, dismantled and reassembled. Later it was owned by a man named Peek Long, who sold unclaimed freight. With a new roof it seems to be in excellent repair.

large deposits of potter's shale and clay for the manufacture of bricks. The Betsey River was said to be capable of furnishing a minimum of 220 horsepower for every mile of its course.

Prospective settlers were assured that good land was available for $2 to $10 an acre, depending on the location. There was a ready market for logs and firewood at good prices; what was left could be sold to the charcoal kilns. Most of the land had enough standing timber to pay for and fence it when cleared.

The editor of the local weekly newspaper declared: "I call to mind a young man who four years ago contracted to buy eighty acres of what we would call stump-land. He had as capital to start with, good health, a young wife with sound judgement, and a team of horses partly paid for. Today he has forty acres cleared, comfortable farm buildings—put up a new barn this season—is out of debt and in five more years, if no bad luck intervenes, will be independent for the rest of his days."

It all sounded pretty rosy, and the people of Thompsonville faced the new century with confidence, convinced that a bright and glorious future was in store.

They were wrong. Thompsonville had no real future at all. The town fathers should have read Shelley's *Ozymandias* to find out what sometimes happens when boasting gets out of hand.

Within five years the sawmills had cut every log available, and the charcoal kilns had gobbled up all that was left. The bare and ravaged forestland was as desolate as a moonscape.

Thompsonville's "Industrial Center" never really got off the ground.

Professor Borradaile was wrong about the soil—it was among the poorest in the state. Through bad management and soil depletion Thompsonville farmers lost the potato market to producers of better quality in Maine, New York, and Idaho.

The area didn't have much to offer tourists, either. They passed it up for the more scenic lake country to the north and east.

The final blow came with the decline of the railroads and their final abandonment in the 1950s and '60s. This put the town in a backwash, miles from the nearest highway. A few houses and empty buildings remain, but in almost every sense of the word, Thompsonville has become a ghost town.

The population figures tell the story: 1900—1,200; 1910—815; 1920—410; 1950—313; 1980—312; 1990—265.

My name is Ozymandias, king of kings:
Look upon my works, ye Mighty, and despair!
Nothing beside remains. Round the decay
Of that colossal wreck, boundless and bare,
The lone and level sands stretch far away.

33
Podunk's Still There

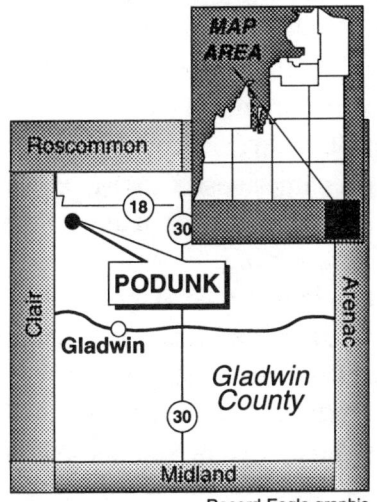
Record-Eagle graphic

No true collector of Michigan ghost towns could possibly resist one with a name like Podunk. Indeed, the word itself is a pretty fair description of most ghost towns—meaning, according to *Webster's Unabridged*, a small town or place of no importance. From the same source one learns that New England has two Podunks and that Podunk is the name of now-extinct Algonquin Indian tribe like James Fenimore Cooper's Mohicans. So much for etymology.

The Podunk School was built in 1904; it was closed down in 1955.

Michigan's Podunk lies in Sage Township in the northwestern quarter of Gladwin County. It's not easy to find. That's because the name doesn't appear on any map less than fifty years old, and even many of the natives seem to have lost track of it.

The best way to get there is to take a right on Bard Road five miles east of Gladwin on M-61; then go four miles north and take another right on Sage Road; then go a mile east and half a mile north on Zeimer Road—and there you are at the ghost town of Podunk. All of it.

You can't miss it because there's an abandoned schoolhouse on one corner and, kitty-corner, an abandoned church. The school was built in 1904 to replace the original log schoolhouse, and was moved to the crossroads in 1918 from its first location half a mile south on Sinclair Hill. The Podunk Free Methodist

Church was built in 1934 or 1935 by volunteer labor. The school's in pretty good shape for its age, but the church has holes in its roof big enough for birds to fly in and out—and they do.

Essentially, Podunk was a church, school, and dancehall, surrounded by farms. It never got big enough for a post office. It never had a railroad, a sawmill, or a grocery store. The nearest stores were three miles away in different directions at Skeels and Oberlin, both of which are now ghost towns, too.

The dancehall was the center of Podunk's social and entertainment life. It stood half a mile west of the crossroads—a big, two-story frame building with a lunchroom upstairs. William Krahmer of Chappel Dam Road says that the dancehall was a pretty wild place.

The Podunk Free Methodist Church was built in 1934 or 1935 and has been unoccupied for at least 30 years.

"We used to get in a fight there nearly every Saturday night," he says. "This was during the days of the Great Depression. There wasn't much else to do at Podunk, and even if there had been, nobody probably could afford it. We paid 35 cents for a ticket to dance. Upstairs we paid 5 cents for coffee and 10 cents for a hamburger. It was a pretty wild place with the fights and all, but I guess it wasn't any wilder than lots of other dancehalls at the time. Everybody brought their own bottle. Most of it was pretty good homemade stuff, moonshine they called it. Anyway, I never heard of anyone that went blind on it."

Podunk was first settled in the late 1860s. Many of the first settlers were farmers who worked in the lumber camps during the winter and early spring. Leslie Hayward, who was born on Gashe Road near Podunk in 1901, said that his father, Charles Hayward, was a river hog.

"He helped drive logs down the Cedar River and the Tobacco River to the Ross Brothers sawmill at Beaverton," Hayward said.

He also said that his father, Matt Smallwood, and O. R. Dow of Pratt Lake built the first road into Podunk. It came up from Pratt Lake. Before that they had only logging roads, Hayward said.

Back to etymology. Hayward said that Podunk was named after a pioneer settler.

"I never heard his first name," Hayward said. "But he had the 40 just east of my place. I was born in 1901 on the 40 just north of Podunk's place."

The dancehall has been gone for over fifty years—Hayward said that it was torn down in 1939. The church hasn't been used for at least thirty years, and the school closed down in 1955. But Podunk's still there. At least in spirit.

34
Mayfield Had Its Ups and Downs

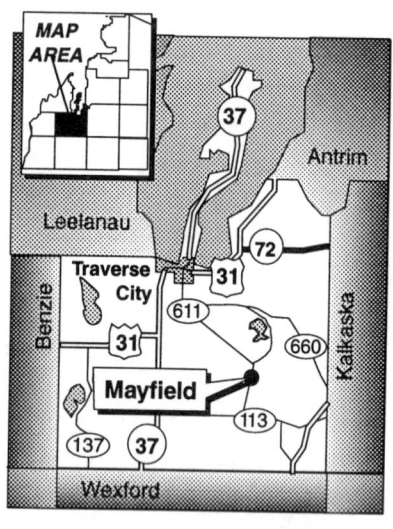

Mayfield is a sleepy little village in the Boardman River valley thirteen miles south of Traverse City. Nothing very exciting has happened there for a long time, and those who remember its close encounters with disaster are mostly dead and gone.

Mayfield's history began in 1866, when two lumbermen from Sheboygan Falls, Wisconsin. George Neal and Lucas Knight, came to the valley and took up timberland claims. They dammed Swainston Creek to make a millpond and built a water-powered sawmill. A year or two later, they built a gristmill below the dam with lumber from the sawmill. The place was first called Beulah.

Two years later, Knight's cousin Lorraine K. Gibbs, came from Wisconsin to join the firm, which was then called Neal, Gibbs & Knight. In 1872, Lorraine's brother, James L. Gibbs, made it a foursome. James also brought his younger brothers, Arch, Frank, and Bird.

Meanwhile, the village acquired a post office in 1869. It was housed in pioneer Charlie Denniston's general store, the first retail business in town. Denniston was the first postmaster, and the town was renamed Mayfield because there was already a Beulah in the area.

The year 1872 also saw the arrival of the first railroad, the Traverse City branch of the Grand Rapids & Indiana, which built a station at Mayfield. That same year the Gibbs brothers bought out Neal and Knight; henceforth the firm did business as Gibbs brothers. It suffered a blow in 1873, when the sawmill burned down, nearly taking the village with it. But the mill was rebuilt in 1874, and that same year the Gibbs also built a new general store, turning the old one into a schoolhouse. Roxa Humphrey was the first teacher.

Mayfield Creek, site of the sawmill.

In 1885, the Gibbs built a new and much larger steam-powered sawmill: it became known far and wide as the Big Red Mill. By that time Mayfield had several stores, a hotel built by Israel Dawdy and called the Dawdy House, two shingle mills in addition to the sawmill, and a population of one hundred.

At 7:05 on the morning of January 8, 1903, the steam boiler at the Big Red Mill blew up with a roar that broke windows, rattled dishes, and tumbled late sleepers out of their beds. Forty-five workers were on duty at the sawmill that morning. Many were blown off their feet and carried some distance—one man was nearly blown into the mill's big circular saw. Only one was seriously injured—engineer Dick Marshall—but he recovered. It seemed a miracle that many more were not killed or seriously hurt.

Several years earlier, James Gibbs had converted the old mill dam into a hydroelectric power plant to supply light and power to the villages of Mayfield and Kingsley. At 4 a.m. on March 24, 1913, the dam washed out after heavy rains, and a ten-foot wall of water swept down the spillway destroying several buildings in its path. It first struck the powerhouse fifty feet below the dam, where engineer John Hawthorne was on duty, and separated into two raging torrents. Hawthorne should've stayed put, for the powerhouse survived the flood. But apparently he panicked, broke for higher ground, and was carried away by the floodwaters. His body, completely stripped of clothing, was found some sixty rods below the dam.

The dam was rebuilt and continued to generate electricity until 1961, when the dam failed again, after several days of torrential rains. This time nobody was hurt, but the waters of the millpond, added to the

Results of the dam washout in 1913. Courtesy of Grand Traverse Pioneer & Historical Society.

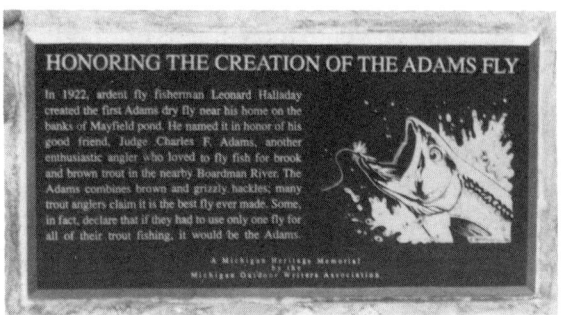

Plaque honoring Leonard Hallady for creation of the Adams trout fly.

already swollen Boardman River, caused a washout of Keystone Dam, seven miles downstream.

In 1985, Lester and Ann Biederman of Traverse City—owners of the pond and twenty acres around it—deeded the property to Paradise Township for a park, now known as Mayfield Pond Park.

Adjacent to it, on the east side of the railroad tracks, is another park donated in 1989 by the Halladay family in commemoration of Leonard and Mary Halladay, whose homestead it was since 1903. A bronze plaque commemorates the creation of the Adams trout fly by Len Halladay in 1922, who named it after his good friend and fellow angler, Judge Charles F. Adams. Made of brown and grizzly bear hackles, it's considered by most fly fisherman as the finest trout fly ever tied.

Mayfield's fortunes declined with the end of timbering. It still has one store and post office and a few resident families; otherwise, it meets most ghost town specifications.

35
Park Lake and
Ghost Creek

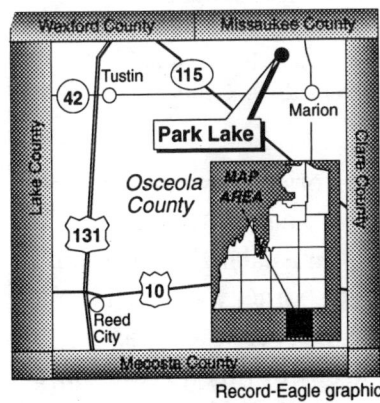
Record-Eagle graphic

Park Lake was a typical sawmill town in Osceola County four miles northwest of Marion on the Ann Arbor Railroad. It traced its origins to a couple named Eliza and Milton Rice, who settled there in the early 1880s and carved out a homestead from the wilderness. A parcel of land they sold in 1887 to Guy Disbrow was the town's first recorded deed. It was given a station on the railroad and, on December 3, 1888, a post office in Disbrow's general store, with Disbrow as postmaster.

Park Lake House around 1905-1908. Loren and Ellen Pardee bought the hotel in 1905. It closed in 1912, and the building was torn down in 1924. Courtesy of Marion Historical Society.

One of the weirdest stories to come out of Park Lake has to do with a man called "Shoot the Cat" Osborne (the origin of his unusual nickname is unfortunately lost to history). Osborne, who lived in Park Lake, was a drinking man. But Park Lake was dry, and the nearest place he could buy a drink was Marion, six miles away by road. It was a little closer by railroad, though, and Osborne got into the habit of walking the tracks to Marion when he ran out of booze. There he'd usually spend the day at the Sample House, one of the many saloons, and then hike the tracks back home that night.

"Shoot the Cat" turned up missing after one of his weekend Marion junkets. A search party, fearing the worst, found his body on the railroad track about two miles north of town. It lay near a trestle over a small unnamed creek that flowed south into the Middle Branch of Muskegon River. It was pretty obvious that he'd been run over by a train.

That wasn't surprising, under the circumstances, but one thing was queer. His shoes and socks were sitting neatly together beside the track. After much speculation it was believed that "Shoot the Cat" was confused. He must have thought he had reached home, and, without a light to guide him, took off his shoes and socks and went to bed on the tracks, ignoring the lumps in the mattress. It was a fatal mistake.

Some time later, an engine crew one night saw a mysterious light hovering over the trestle across the creek, near the spot where "Shoot the Cat" met his untimely end. It moved erratically up and down, they said, and from side to side, then drifted along the creek

This old house was originally the Park Lake post office.

Old house at Park Lake.

The grave of Chief Petoskey's grandson at Park Lake Cemetery.

and vanished into a nearby woods. Another crew said they saw the same thing a few nights later. And then the word got around that it must be "Shoot the Cat's" ghost, carrying a lantern to look for his shoes and socks. Anyway that's how Ghost Creek got its name.

The big pine timber was gone before Park Lake got started, and it took another ten or fifteen years before the hardwood was finished, too. Park Lake lasted that long but not much longer. Now only one house (said to be the old post office) and the cemetery remain.

It's a picturesque little graveyard on a little knoll south of town. It contains the graves of most of the Park Lake pioneers, including that of James Kingsley Petoskey—grandson of Chippewa Indian Chief Petoskey—and his wife Elizabeth Helmboldt.

36
Crofton Was a Hard Luck Town

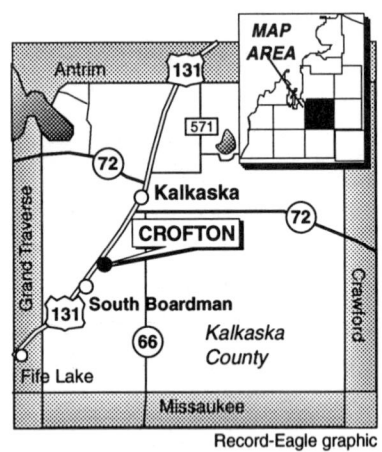

Record-Eagle graphic

Many hopeful Michigan villages met up with hard luck of one kind or another and perished. Crofton seems to have had more than its share.

Crofton was one of a half dozen villages that sprang up along the Grand Rapids and Indiana Railroad when it came through Kalkaska County in 1872 on its way to Petoskey. It got its start in 1875, when the firm of Meek, Junk and Hiatt built a sawmill there and started timbering operations along the North Branch of the Boardman River. The village was platted in 1877, and that same year it was almost totally destroyed by fire—the sawmill, boarding house, general store, and three or four dwellings all went up in flames.

Not daunted, the reorganized firm of Meek, Harper and Duthie immediately rebuilt the mill and the town, which was platted anew a year or two later. In 1884, *The Traverse Region* (Chicago, 1884) quoted a story that had appeared in one of the area's local newspapers in May of 1878. The story, somewhat abridged, is as follows:

> "Less than a year ago Crofton was almost entirely burned. With characteristic enterprise the proprietors, Messrs. Meek, Harper, and Duthie immediately rebuilt the mill and put it in operation. There are now about twenty-five buildings. About one million feet of lumber have been shipped to the southern market since the first of March. Fifty-one carloads were shipped in the month of April alone. The sawmill is in operation around the clock, and twelve teams of horses are required to supply the logs. Between thirty and forty men are employed. There is a large store, owned by the proprietors of the town, a large hotel or boarding house, several dwelling houses, and a post office."

Crofton depot on the Grand Rapids & Indiana Railroad. Section crew in foreground. Courtesy of Phebe Cotton Collection.

The post office was granted in 1875, and John F. Hiatt was its first postmaster.

The Traverse Region's account, however, ends on a somewhat melancholy note: "*Since that time the village has rather gone backward, and there is but little business done at the present time.*"

As if to confirm that report, Crofton lost its post office in 1884. But it was restored in 1886, and continued in operation until 1909.

Crofton seems to have found a new lease on life in 1890, when Charles Stites built a shingle mill there. This brought an influx of a colorful group of men known as "shingle weavers." They wore gaudy bib overalls and rolled but not stagged pants, brightly colored shirts, and white or vividly colored hats.

John Ives, who grew up in Crofton, was quoted as saying: "You could always spot a shingle weaver—and not only by his dress. He usually had fingers missing on both hands. A weaver with both thumbs was a rarity." The froe used by shingle weavers was sharp as a razor, and just one slip could result in lost fingers.

A major tragedy struck the town in 1887 with the outbreak of a diptheria epidemic. So great was the fear of contagion that the trainmen of the GR & I refused to stop at the depot and all goods and supplies were unloaded a mile or two down the tracks.

The epidemic raged for only three or four weeks, but it took a fearful toll. People stricken with the disease were ill only a day or two before they died. It was said that only four or five of the town's children survived. And that perhaps more than anything else, took the heart out of the survivors and spelt Crofton's doom.

The old Crofton one-room school, now a residence, is all that's left of the village.

Today, open fields on both sides of the railroad tracks near US-131, five miles south of Kalkaska, show where the village once stood—and a single relic, the old school, which is now a residence, still stands.

An interesting but rather fanciful story is told about how Crofton got its name. In 1868, a young man named Tom Crofton was running traplines on the river near the site of Crofton. He shot a deer for food, but when he approached to dress it, the animal reared up and pinned him against the trunk of a big white pine, breaking his leg. He managed to apply a crude splint to the break and to survive the winter by building a rough lean-to and living on venison and beaver meat. He was found next spring, more dead than alive, by a passing band of Indians, who carried him to the small town of Fife Lake.

Legend has it that Crofton was named after him, but evidently there is little truth to the story. Records show that it was named for a pioneer settler, E. Crofton Fox, who sold the land to the lumber company. Fife Lake wasn't settled until 1872; it was wilderness until then.

History has a nasty way of spoiling a good story.

37
Mitchell Had a Grist Mill

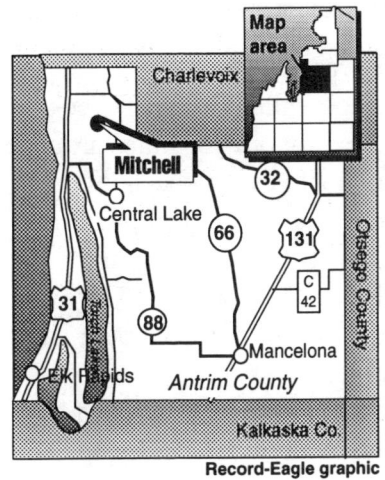

Record-Eagle graphic

Mitchell, near the center of Banks Township in Antrim County, is different from the average, run-of-the-mill Michigan ghost town. It grew up around a grist mill instead of a sawmill or a mine. Later, it had a sawmill, too, but it was small potatoes compared with Central Lake Lumber Company's giant steam mill on King Creek at Essex, less than a mile away.

The Wiltse homestead on Mitchell Road with one of Ed Wiltse's horses in silhouette.

Mitchell's gristmill was built by pioneer Edward Wiltse on Wiltse Creek (now called Ogletree Creek) in the late 1860s. It was the only one for miles around. Grandson Ed Wiltse, who lives on the homestead farm, remembers his father Ralph telling how farmers from the Central Lake area brought their grain to the mill up the "Chain O' Lakes" in rowboats. The overland trip from Central Lake or farther south took twenty-four hours or more.

Ed's grandfather landed at Antrim City around 1867 and came overland with his family, household goods, and farm animals to his 16-acre homestead near what soon became the village of Mitchell. John McNeill became its first postmaster in 1869; Edward Wiltse was appointed postmaster in 1876. Other postmasters were Samuel Walton, Ralph Wiltse, and Mrs. W. Wiltse.

The first log school was opened in 1872, and the records show that twenty pupils were in attendance. Eventually, as many as twenty-five families were served by the Mitchell post office and school. The school was called a "three-month school" because the big boys and girls went to school for three months in the winter, and the smaller ones for three months in the summer.

Among the school documents that have survived—including some of the minutes of the school board meetings—is the Mitchell School Teachers contract for 1902:

1. *Not to get married. This contract becomes null and void if the teacher marries.*
2. *Not to have company with men.*
3. *To be home between the hours of eight pm and six am unless in attendance at a school function.*
4. *Not to loiter downtown in ice cream store.*
5. *Not to leave town at any time without the permission of the chairman of the trustees.*
6. *Not to smoke cigarettes.*
7. *Not to drink beer, wine or whiskey.*
8. *Not to ride in a carriage or automobile with any man except her brother or father.*
9. *Not to dress in bright colors.*
10. *Not to dye her hair.*
11. *To wear at least two petticoats.*
12. *Not to wear dresses more than two inches above ankles.*

13. To keep the schoolroom clean.
    a. Sweep the classroom floor once daily.
    b. Scrub classroom floor once weekly with soap and hot water.
    c. Clean blackboard at least once daily.
    d. To start fire at seven am so that the room will be warm at eight am when the children arrive.
14. Not to wear face powder, mascara or to paint the lips.

In 1902, a local newspaper reported that the Mitchell school had over fifty pupils and a new well. Legend has it that one of the school teachers hanged herself from a tree behind the school. Details are

The mill pond at Mitchell used to be around sixteen feet deep. Now, filled with lilypads, giant bullfrogs, and tons of slabwood on the bottom, it's only about three or four feet deep.

lacking, but one wonders what rule of the teachers contract she broke, if any—or something worse?

The Mitchell post office closed in 1902, but the school, rebuilt at least twice, remained in operation until 1941.

Now all that's left of the town of Mitchell is the mill pond, the remains of the old earthen dam, and two huge millstones half hidden in the tall grass.

One of the two big millstones from the gristmill on Wiltse Creek (now Ogletree Creek) at Mitchell. It's about four feet in diameter, one-and-one-half feet thick and girdled by a heavy iron hoop one foot wide and an inch thick.

38
South Boardman Was Crippled By Fire

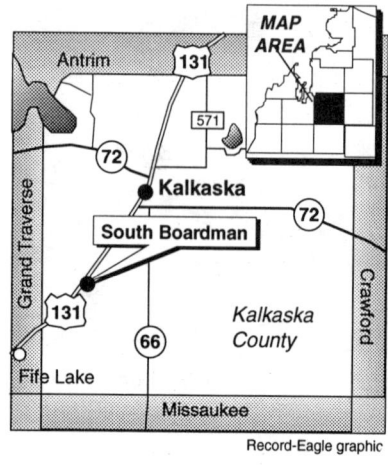
Record-Eagle graphic

South Boardman in Kalkaska County, eight miles southwest of the village of Kalkaska, is one of the pleasantest ghost towns in northern lower Michigan. A river runs through it—the south branch of the Boardman River—and the town embraces a fifteen- or twenty-acre mill pond behind a dam that was built in 1878 to power the first sawmill. South Boardman has the charm of an English

Ruins of South Boardman after the big fire of 1921. Courtesy of Phebe Cotton.

river village on the Avon or the Cam except that there are few large shade trees and no houses or buildings more than a century old.

That's because the great fire of 1921 left the whole town in a heap of smouldering ruins. South Boardman had several major fires before that, but the fire of 1921 was the big one from which the town never fully recovered.

The town got started in 1874 when Hamilton Stone of Ovid, Michigan came up on the Grand Rapids and Indiana Railroad to commence lumbering operations. Stone had been told by a friend, pioneer Orange A. Row, that there was a stand of eighty acres of big pine timber near the crossing of the railroad and the south branch of the Boardman River. Stone and several other men arrived there at sundown in the fall of

Above: Anderson sawmill, destroyed by fire in 1910. Courtesy of Phebe Cotton.

Right: South Boardman's old depot, destroyed in the 1921 fire. Courtesy of Phebe Cotton Collection.

Left: South Boardman's new depot on the Grand Rapids & Indiana Railroad is now a residence. Only about half of the original building now remains.

1874. They proceeded to build a shanty with some lumber they'd brought with them, cooked supper, built a big fire at the open end of their shanty, and took turns tending it during the night. Two of the men were Orange Row and John D. Dagle.

Stone went on to build a dam in 1877 and a sawmill in 1878. The dam provided a fall of ten feet at the mill and plenty of power for the single muley saw, which was soon replaced by a more efficient circular one. The capacity of the mill was thus increased from 2,000 board feet to 15,000 a day. Stone also built the first hotel, known as the Boardman River House, and depot of the GR & I.

In the summer of 1875 Frank P. Smith moved his goods from Fife Lake and opened a general store in a building next to the hotel. The town was awarded a post office in 1875 with George W. Briggs as the first postmaster. He was replaced the following year by Frank P. Smith, who moved the office into his store. The first school was also built in 1875.

The town really began to boom in 1883, when J. L. Quimby of Grand Rapids and M. B. Farrin of Cincinnati built large steam sawmills there. The population in 1870 was 172; in 1883 it had increased to 367. By 1902 the town had four sawmills, a gristmill, two shingle mills, a handle factory, a butterbowl factory, a cement factory and a creamery, as well as many other businesses. It also had three lumbercamps in the vicinity, a couple of boarding houses, four hotels, four churches, and five saloons. A newspaper, the *Boardman River Current*, was established in 1901.

The first big fire took place in 1905, when the Burlson Hotel burned down. It was never rebuilt.

In 1910, the Anderson sawmill was destroyed by fire and never rebuilt.

In 1911, an entire business block, including a hardware, undertaking parlor, bakery, restaurant, saloon, furniture store, meat market, boarding house, and opera house went up in flames. None was ever rebuilt.

The big fire of 1921 started on the roof of Dan Flannigan's Barber Shop and Pool Hall. It burned north through Atkin's Hotel and Restaurant, Wakefield's General Store, Brett's Building, J. J. Neihardt's Drugstore, the post office, South Boardman Gleaner's Produce Company, and F. Glendenning's shoe shop, as well as many of the homes.

Horse-and-buggy with South Boardman Baptist Church in background. Around 1910. Courtesy of Phebe Cotton Collection.

The old South Boardman post office, now an historical museum, was built after the fire of 1921. It was moved across the street from its original location (which is now occupied by the new post office).

And that, for all practical purposes, was the end of South Boardman as a living village.

A brave attempt at resuscitation was made in 1930, when the city fathers filed corporation papers and South Boardman became the smallest incorporated village in America. Alas, it was not for long. The corporation was voted out in 1932.

39
Pennock and the Railroad War

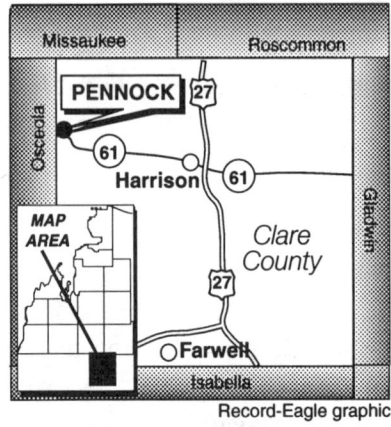
Record-Eagle graphic

Pennock—or Pennock Siding as it was sometimes called—didn't last long but had a colorful career while it lasted. On the Ann Arbor and Toledo Railroad in northwestern Clare County, Pennock was one of serveral villages that were born in 1887, when the railroad was building from Farwell to Marion.

The coming of the railroad was an exciting event in this sparsely populated area. What made it even more exciting was the war between the railroad and the settlers.

Two pioneer families were involved, the Luxes and the Chapins. Joseph Lux and Ira Chapin had bought land on the projected railway route in the hope of cashing in big on the sale of rights of way. Lux, on the advice of his lawyer, had even built a log house in its path. Both men, however, failed to reckon on James M. Ashley, the builder of the railroad.

Ashley, a former governor of Montana and member of Congress, had the build of a professional football tackle and the temperament of a buccaneer. In building his railroad he acquired most rights of way for nothing and ignored the holdouts by building his railroad across their land and letting the lawyers fight it out in court. Seldom, if ever, did he have to pay a

The Pennock barrel stave and shingle factory stood in the open field at the left.

judgement. His son and partner in the enterprise, James Ashley, Jr. said later that he could write a book entitled *How to Build 600 Miles of Railroad without a Damned Cent*.

The war was fought between the railroad workers armed mostly with picks and shovels and the settlers with rifles and shotguns. Casualties were few, but one worker lost his life and Ira Chapin had his leg shot off. The railroad went through. Lux got a small settlement. Chapin got nothing.

At its best Pennock consisted only of two rows of houses on its main street (which is now Kirby Road, devoid of houses), the Lux and Florin general store, a rooming house, dance hall and baseball diamond, but no saloon. All the men worked at the big sawmill across the tracks. By this time, the pine was long gone, and the mill turned out nothing but elm barrel staves and cedar shingles. There was also a school and a post office, granted in 1892, with Thomas J. Flevens as postmaster.

Pennock had its beginning in violence and it ended in violence—a particularly gruesome murder. It happened in 1913.

The victim, Harry Crill, was a sometime fur trader and cattle dealer. He was also a self-confessed drunkard. Since Pennock was dry, Crill had to walk the railroad tracks three miles to Temple for his booze and, like "Shoot the Cat" Osborne of Park Lake, he was usually dead drunk when he made the return trip. One Pennock oldtimer remembered coming upon Crill on his hands and knees, crawling across the trestle railroad bridge over Giss-I-Wass Creek one evening.

"Do you need help?" he asked him.

"What help is there for a drunk?" responded Crill.

Legend has it that Crill's Indian wife Mary killed him with an axe as he lay in a drunken stupor on the sandy path leading from the railroad tracks to his cabin. But the facts are somewhat less dramatic. According to court records of the trial of Mary Crill for murder, she dispatched him with a hatchet while he lay passed out in his bed after a drunken family brawl. Mary was nevertheless acquitted. One Pennock man explained the jury's verdict by saying that it was a crime to give an Indian liquor; therefore Crill deserved what he got.

The spot where legend has it that Mary Grill slew her husband with an axe.

The Pennock schoolhouse serves as a residence in Temple today.

Pennock went rapidly downhill after the elm and the cedar were gone. It lost its post office in 1907, and in 1937 the abandoned schoolhouse was moved to Temple, where it still serves as a residence. Now nothing at all is left of Pennock, not even a stone on stone—it's as if the village had been wiped from the face of the earth.

40
Williamsburg Had a Gas Blowout

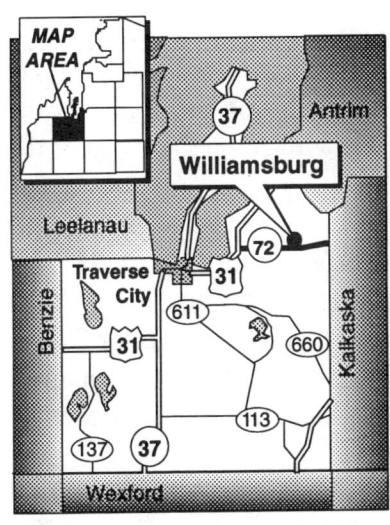

Williamsburg in eastern Grand Traverse County is arguably the most beautiful ghost town in Michigan. A pretty little creek runs through it—once called Mill Creek, now Williamsburg Creek—and the creek was dammed in the late 1850s to provide power for Truman Scofield's grist mill, which still stands.

Williamsburg mill pond.

With its placid, tree-shaded mill pond, lovely and well-preserved old homes and giant shade trees, Williamsburg—in mild contrast to South Boardman in Kalkaska County—has all, not just some of, the charm of an English river village on the Avon or the Cam.

Williamsburg had three names before finally settling on the fourth. The original settlers called it Mill Creek after the stream that flows through it. In 1867 it was given a post office as Dunbar, named for Eber J. Dunbar, its first postmaster. In 1869 it was renamed Williamsburgh, and in 1894 this was shortened to Williamsburg.

The original settlers were three families from Monroe County, New York, who came here in 1856. History unfortunately, has not preserved their names.

Around 1880, the village acquired a steam sawmill, which A. W. Eaton, David Vinton, and Kossuth

Stites built just east of town on the site of an artesian flowing well, which supplied the mill with plenty of water. It is said that the mill machinery was shipped by rail to Traverse City from Kalamazoo, then to Williamsburg by a team of horses.

The business section of town was moved a quarter mile north to old M-72 when the Chicago and West Michigan (later Chesapeake and Ohio) came through in 1890.

Probably the most dramatic thing that ever happened to Williamsburg was the blowout of 1973.

In the early evening of April 18 of that year, Williamsburg resident Margaret Beckwith had just returned from a visit to the hospital when her daughter and son-in-law arrived.

"Where'd that big hole in the back yard come from?" they asked her. She thought they were kidding

The old Truman Scofield's grist mill on the Williamsburg mill pond, built late 1850s.

Whitewater Township Hall at Williamsburg, built 1889.

but went to look and found a big hole in the ground just off the back porch. It was in the same spot where an artesian well had dried up and been filled in.

Mrs. Beckwith summoned a state policeman, who told her to turn off the furnace and vacate the property immediately. She went to her daughter's house on M-72 not far away, and at three a.m. there was a knock on the door. A new crater had opened near the daughter's house and was spewing out gas, water and mud. The police officer told them to turn off the power and evacuate at once. That night many other Williamsburg people were told to vacate their homes.

Today it is clear that the eruptions were caused by an underground blowout at an Amoco gas well four miles south of Williamsburg. Natural gas had leaked through a crack on the drilling shaft and seeped into the porous limestone rock and then into the groundwater.

High pressure had pushed the gas to the Williamsburg area where it erupted through water wells, abandoned test wells, and streams. One eruption undermined a whole section of M-72 and closed the highway for weeks.

Meanwhile, a general state of emergency was declared. During the next few days almost one hundred families were evacuated, and the entire village was cordoned off. The greatest danger lay in possible explosions of natural gas which had reached combustible levels in the atmosphere.

The state of emergency lasted one hundred days. It was finally brought under control by Amoco workers

Williamsburg United Methodist Church. It was built in 1881.

Millbrook mansion at Williamsburg.

who plugged the broken drill shaft with concrete, drilled several relief holes south of the village, and filled in most of the blowholes. Later, Amoco had to drill fifty-four new water wells for the residents—water from the old ones wasn't fit to drink. But it was months, even years in some cases, before all the Williamsburg people could return to their homes.

Today, only memories of the blowout remain, and Williamsburg has resumed its tranquil, almost idyllic existence. Its "jewel in the crown" is Millbrook, which includes the old dam and gristmill and much of the mill pond frontage. Over the years, its lovely white Colonial mansion has been home to many prominent Traverse area families, including Charles and Laura Scofield (1867-1905), Dr. Benjamin and Olga Bushong (1952-1967), and Fitch and Louise Williams (1967-1979).

Other landmarks include the United Methodist Church (1881) and Whitewater Township Hall (1889).

41
The Indians Called It Wekwagamaw

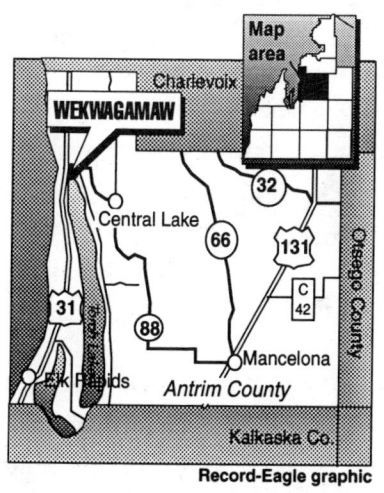

Few people today are old enough to remember the Ottawa Indian village three miles north of Elk Rapids at the tip of Elk Lake. White people called it Indiantown. The Indians called it Wekwagamaw, which very loosely translated means "the bay at the end of the lake." There used to be a sign with that name on it to mark the site, but that's gone now and so is the village, although two or three Indian families still live in the neighborhood.

The Kewaydin United Methodist Mission Church lies on the old Wekwagamaw indian village site.

Nobody knew how long the village had been there. But there were Ottawas in Michigan long before Columbus "discovered" America. And since the village lay on a branch of the Mackinaw Trail, paleo-Indians probably camped there for several thousand years.

In February 1884, the *Elk Rapids Progress* reported the death of Kewaydin (North Wind) chief of the band at Wekwagamaw, after whom the present village was named.

Nobody knew the chief's age, either, but he must have been crowding 100 if it was true, as he said, that he had served against the British under head chief Aishquagwonaba in the War of 1812, participating in the massacre of River Raisin. Kewaydin was the greatest hunter and trapper in the region. Regularly each spring he would show up with a pack of furs twice as large as anyone else's. Kewaydin was also a witch doctor and sorcerer. In his medicine chest were the skins of eight species of snakes, plus toads and lizards, and a stuffed beaver, which he said, upon being fed the "bad medicine" made from the crawly things, would snort fire from its nostrils and scoot along the floor.

The chief's word was law. For people he wished to punish he had a hex that never failed. He'd draw a picture of the offender on birch bark, then smear an arrowhead with the "bad medicine" and stab the point of it into the heart or head of the culprit's image, thus killing or driving him crazy. But the chief was a benevolent dictator and only exercised such powers

The Indian cemetery behind the church.

when the nature of the crime warranted. His people feared him, but they also liked and respected him.

Kewaydin had a traditional Indian funeral with "modern" trimmings. He lay neatly dressed in an open coffin along with artifical flowers, his hunting knife, a small quantity of corn for seed in the spirit land, two extra white linen collars in case the one he wore became soiled on the expected four days' journey, cotton cloth for a tent, and, most curious of all, a long leather strap with a hook attached. The latter was for use for scaling the walls of the "celestial city" if he was refused admittance.

With regard to the strap and hook for climbing the walls to heaven, the *Elk Rapids Progress* story had this to say:

"There is many a man deems himself among the elect who would do well to imitate this custom, for many will need a longer strap than poor old untutored Kewaydin."

44
Stittsville Had Hopes

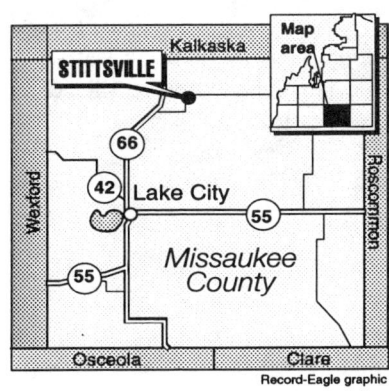
Record-Eagle graphic

Stittsville had high hopes of becoming (after Lake City) the second biggest town in Missaukee County. Its hopes were pinned on the coming of a railroad. There were four possibilities. One, that the J. Henry Moores Lumber Company of Moorestown would extend its West Branch and Moorestown logging railroad three miles from Moorestown to Stittsville. Two, that the Pere Marquette Railroad could be persuaded to extend its Rapid City-Kalkaska branch from Stratford to Stittsville. Three, that the Mitchell Brothers of Cadillac

Stittsville Hotel and Saloon, built in 1898, by Nathan Doherty. The Hotel was torn down and the lumber shipped to Lansing in 1916. Courtesy of Howard Yount.

would build a logging railroad to the village from its big sawmill headquarters at Jennings. And four, that the Grand Rapids and Indiana Railroad would extend its Missuakee Branch from Lake City to Stittsville.

There is good reason to believe that one of the possibilities would materialize, for the Stittsville area had one of the biggest stands of virgin pine still left in lower Michigan. It included a giant record-setting white pine that measured seventeen feet around the base at stump height and was estimated to contain 7,000 board feet of lumber.

Stittsville had to wait more than a decade for its railroad, but it finally arrived. In 1898 Mitchell Brothers built a narrow-gauge railroad from Jennings through

Morey on present M-66 northeast to their lumbercamp 29, half a mile from Stittsville.

The village was first settled around 1875 by several members of the Stitts family, who hailed from Stittsville, Canada. Located on the old Houghton Lake-Traverse City State Road, it was granted a post office as Norwich (the name of the township) in 1879, with Orlando C. Gorthy as postmaster. He was succeeded in 1885 by John T. Stitt, and the office was renamed for him.

Stittsville indeed boomed with the coming of the railroad. Mitchell Brothers built a big general store, the biggest in the county before or since. There was a hardware store owned by Miles E. Stitts, two hotels, a drugstore, two blacksmithies, a big livery stable, and a saloon. The lumber camps, scattered in all directions

Stittsville store in 1898. Courtesy of Howard Yount.

Giant record-setting white pine near Stittsville. Courtesy of Howard Yount.

around the town, employed hundreds of men, who came to town on weekends and turned it into a replica of the Wild West.

Unfortunately, the boom lasted only about six years. By 1904, the big timber was gone and the railroad pulled out. Some of the houses were moved to nearby farms or pulled down for lumber. Some of the buildings burned. Now only the old United Methodist Church and the Stittsville Cemetery remain.

In 1928, despite a movement to preserve it, Stittsville's giant white pine—said to be 700 years old—was cut down by lumberman logging the area. One of its biggest logs was on display at a Lake City park for several years, but then it too disappeared.

One of the many stories in connection with Stittsville reflects the racial prejudice so wide-spread in those days and by no means uncommon in these.

In April 1897, officials of the Grand Rapids and Indiana Railroad came to Lake City in their private car and were then driven by horse-and-buggy to Stittsville to look over the prospects for an extension of the Missuakee Branch. While they were gone, a black cook employed in the private railroad car took a stroll about town to see the sights. In the course of his ramble, he came upon some Indians and bought a couple of baskets to take home as souvenirs. As he passed the schoolhouse, a Mrs. C. L. Goll mistook him for an Indian and asked how much he wanted for the baskets.

"Pardon me, ma'am," he said, lifting his cap, "but I would prefer that you regard me as a buyer, not a seller."

Stittsville's United Methodist church today.

The Stittsville cemetery.

Later, he told the trainmen, "Lordy, lordy, what kind of people we got around here? It's bad enough to be colored without being taken for a common redskin."

The story, in different form, was printed in the Lake City *Plain Dealer* on April 21, 1897. The proposed railroad extension was never built.

43
Springvale Went from Rags to Riches

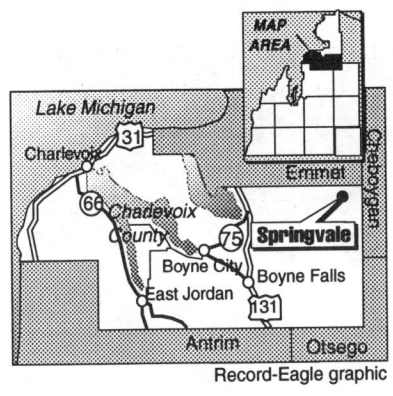
Record-Eagle graphic

You'd have a hard time finding a lonelier place than Springvale. It lies on Springvale Road twelve miles east of Walloon Lake in the northeastern corner of Charlevoix's Chandler Township. It's situated at the intersection of three dirt roads, two of which were old logging trails. A logging railroad also intersects the area, but the rails and ties are long gone and no train has stopped there in almost one hundred years.

Overview of Springvale. General store in foreground. Courtesy of Charlie Conn.

All that's left of the village are the usual vestiges that most ghost towns leave behind—ruined foundation walls and basement depressions where buildings once stood. Yet Springvale was once a busy railroad town and the headquarters for Cobbs and Mitchell's logging operations in the area.

It all began in 1879 when the Cadillac firm of Jonathon W. Cobbs and George A. Mitchell began to build a standard-gauge railroad from Boyne Falls into the wilderness of eastern Charlevoix and Cheboygan counties, where it owned 40,000 acres of hardwood timber. The railroad, which they called the Boyne Falls and Northeastern, eventually consisted of almost one hundred miles of track, and at one point was within three-and-one-half miles of Wolverine and a connection with the Michigan Central Railroad, which was considered but not pursued.

That same year they built the town of Springvale, twelve miles northeast of Boyne Falls. It had a roundhouse, a hotel with sixteen rooms, a big two-story general store, 54' by 160', and a post office with store keeper George Mohorter as postmaster. Both the store and the hotel were steam heated and lighted by gas.

The company ran two trains of logs each day to Boyne Falls. Since the last one returned late at night, a midnight meal was provided for the train crew. By this time, logging had become pretty sophisticated and efficient. The logs were loaded aboard flatcars by McGiffert loaders—of which the company had two—as fast as they could be skidded out of the woods. The

Cobbs & Mitchell's Alco locomotive No. 9 at Springvale. Courtesy of Charlie Conn.

machine was self-propelled and had a winch to pull the cars into position. The average flatcar could be loaded with logs in about ten minutes.

The Cobbs and Mitchell logging camps were models of their kind. They were clean and comfortable, and the beds had springs and mattresses. Sheets and pillow cases were washed once a week. All bunk houses, cook shanties, and other camp buildings were fumigated regularly with steam jets from the locomotives.

But everything comes to an end, sooner or later, and Springvale had no good reason for existence after the timber was gone. Most of the village was torn down in 1925. Two small buildings remained standing until a few years ago when a natural gas supply line went through and obliterated them, too.

Now nothing remains at the lonely crossroads except a seemingly superfluous stop sign. The scene calls to mind Walter de le Mare's lone horseman riding up to an old house in the moonlight and calling out, "Is anyone there?" and calling again without a response, then riding on as "the silence surged softly backward, when the plunging hoofs were gone."

Jonathon Cobbs of Cobbs and Mitchell died in 1898. His grave in Cadillac's Maple Wood Cemetery is marked by a shaft of beautifully polished dark Quincy granite, four feet wide at the base, eleven feet tall, and costing $800.

This sparked a competition among Cadillac lumber barons and their progeny to see who could build the biggest, most elaborate, and most expensive monument in the cemetery. The outcome was a tie between William W. Mitchell, whose monument is larger and

The lonely crossroads at Springvale.

Fred and Carrie Diggins being escorted into heaven by their guardian angel.

stands at the very pinnacle of cemetery hill, looking down on all the others, and Fred A. Diggins, whose life-size figures of himself and his wife—plus a guardian angel as a guide—all cast in bronze, probably were more expensive. Both Diggins and his wife Carrie died a few months apart, in 1914.

William W. Mitchell's monument in Cadillac's Maple Wood Cemetary.

One wonders if all these tycoons were acting in defiance of or maybe just in ignorance of Jesus Christ's admonition (*Matthew 19:24*) about rich men and camels. Let's be charitable and give them the benefit of the doubt.

44
Falmouth and the Ancient Indian Village

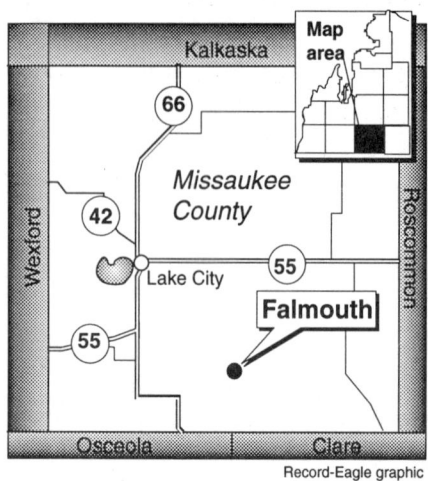
Record-Eagle graphic

Falmouth in south central Missuakee County eighteen miles east of Cadillac isn't really a ghost town. Although only a handful of people still live there, it has a substantial business establishment—including two restaurants—that serves a widespread community of prosperous farms in the Clam River watershed. It therefore seems a good bet to hang in there for a good many years to come.

Falmouth, an old lumbering settlement in Clam River Township, was first called Pen Hook. Eugene W. Watson became its first postmaster in 1871, when the office was named Falmouth. At that time, Falmouth and Reeder (now Lake City) were the only settlements of any size in the county. In 1873, in one of northern Michigan's many courthouse battles (this one never actually came to blows) Falmouth came within one vote of beating out Reeder for the county seat. Falmouth was served by a branch of the Grand Rapids and Indiana Railroad as long as the timber lasted.

Why all this about a place that doesn't qualify as a ghost town?

Because Falmouth is neighbor to one of the oldest ghost towns in Michigan. Falmouth is about 130 years old. The prehistoric no-name indian village, three miles west of Falmouth in Riverside Township, is at

The hay field on Bob Boven's farm, site of the old Indian village.

Mosquito Creek near the old village.

least 800 and maybe more than 1,200 years old. In any case, it was a thriving village long before Columbus ever set foot on this continent.

The site of the ancient village is now a hay field on the back forty of Bob Boven's dairy farm. It's a roughly circular piece of land, with a diameter of about 165 feet, and it's enclosed by a moat or ditch. The ditch is about twelve feet wide and four or five feet deep, and considering 1,000 years of erosion, it must originally have been at least twice or three times deeper—a formidable obstacle to potential mischief-makers, man or beast.

Indeed, many archeologists believe that the earthwork was a kind of fort or stockade. In addition to the moat, the village was also surrounded by a palisade, a solid fence of poles around the inner side of the ditch, in an embankment of the earth removed from the ditch.

Little is known about these people—except that they were not the same Indians that European explorers found living in Michigan in the sixteenth century: Ottawas, Chippewas and Potawatomies. Similar earthworks have been found all over lower Michigan, most of them circular, a few, rectilinear. Many more must have been obliterated by erosion and the plow. There are two of them in nearby Aetna Township, and four on the Rifle River in Ogema County forty miles away. All were obviously built by the same people.

And then they disappeared. All the sites seem to have been abandoned at about the same time, around AD 1400. Possibly they were driven out by other tribes or maybe they moved out voluntarily because of a change in the climate—Michigan turned much colder about that time.

Bob Boven in the ditch surrounding the village site.

A few pieces from Bob Boven's collection.

Since 1928, the site, known among Michigan archeologists as the Boven Earthworks, has been subjected to a few piecemeal digs, most recently by a team under Charles Cleland of Michigan State University twenty-five years ago. The artifacts unearthed in that excavation—stone tools, arrowheads, axes, bannerstones and pottery—are now on display at MSU.

Boven has a small collection of his own, picked up during a lifetime of trapping on Mosquito Creek, which runs through his property and borders the old Indian village. He was born on this well-kept farm and says with a chuckle that he'll probably die on it.

He often thinks about those people who lived on the property a thousand years ago. As a hunter and trapper he feels a close bond of kinship with them. Mosquito Creek is a good mink creek, he says, and there's lots of game in the area. "A few nights ago we counted seventy-five deer in that field across the road."

Boven wonders what kind of people will be living here a thousand years from now, and if the game will be as plentiful and the trapping as good. He hopes they will be lovers of the land, content to share it with all living things, as he and those long-gone villagers have done.

45
Stover on the River

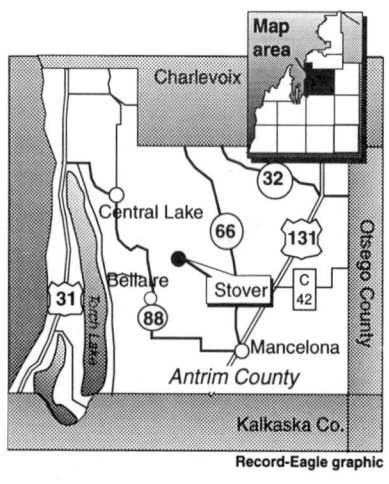
Record-Eagle graphic

Cedar River rises in the hills of Antrim County a few miles east of Bellaire. In the steep valley on the east side of so-called Schuss Mountain it runs fast over cobblestone and sand, and seven miles later empties into the waterway between Lake Bellaire and Intermediate Lake. Most of the way it's much too shallow for canoeing, but there are a few pools where the fish can lounge, and the river is said to be good water for brook trout.

The ghost town of Stover lies in the river valley just east of Schuss Mountain Resort, on a road that used to be called Stover Road but has since been renamed Schuss Mountain Road over the bitter protests of oldtimers in the area, to whom it will always be Stover Road and nothing else. They remember skiing down the "mountain," dodging trees on wooden skis with a single narrow leather strap for a binding, and deplore these decadent days when a good ski outfit—skis, boots, bindings and and poles, to say nothing of the proper attire—can cost upwards of a thousand dollars.

In this snug river valley in 1875, a settlement formed around the lumber mill of Stover, Hay & Company. Power for the mill was supplied by a wide earthen dam that extended the full width of the valley and formed a good-sized body of water known as Stover Pond. Edgar W. Rose built a general store on

Cedar River at Stover.

The Stover house.

the west side of the river and was named postmaster on April 28, 1880. The upstairs of the building was used for Sunday school classes, dancing and other social gatherings.

After the sawmill shut down for want of timber, G. S. Stover built a wood-working shop on the west end of the dam. He used a lathe powered by a water wheel to produce small wooden bowls that were used by grocers to dispense butter and lard. Later, Henry Hull of Mancelona and Traverse City produced them in great quantity and they were known as oval wood dishes—the universal disposable containers of their day.

Stover later transferred his operation to the east end of the dam, where William Ingalls had built a grist mill, a three-story building with vertical siding and wood battens. Water was diverted by a wooden flume to a water wheel under the center of the building, supplying power to the grinding stone.

In 1886, Milton Stover built a home, and it still stands as part of the present house facing the earthen dam. By the turn of the century Stover was a thriving village with a blacksmith shop and an Assembly of God Church in addition to the store and the mill.

In 1904, Dr. John Verdier, A. S. Culbertson and his son Verne acquired Stover's rights on the river and founded the Antrim Power and Illuminating Company. They rebuilt the dam, reinforced it with concrete, and installed a single inlet, double-outlet Wheeler turbine connected with a 200 kilowatt generator. They also built a transmission line to the village of Mancelona.

Until 1895, the streets of Mancelona had been lighted by kerosene lanterns. An official lamplighter lit the lamps each evening and blew them out in the

The remnants of the Stover dam showing the single-inlet turbine housing on the south side.

Remants of the Stover dam with the double-outlet turbine housing.

morning. Later, Mancelona had a small steam generating plant that furnished enough electricity for five 1500-candle-power arc street lights. Four of these turned off at midnight to save money, leaving one to burn all night.

The Antrim Light and Illuminating Company served Mancelona with dependable electricity until the depression years of the thirties, when the street lights were disconnected because the village couldn't pay the light bill.

Michigan Public Service acquired the dam in 1913 or thereabouts, and operated it until it was taken over by Consumers Power Company, which phased it out after a short time. The dam was washed out in the heavy spring rains of 1967, and Stover Pond is no more.

Neither is Stover. It lost its post office in 1888, and like the Cheshire Cat, gradually disappeared, leaving only the remnants of the dam and the Stover house to mark the place where it once stood.

46
Growing up at Fiborn Quarry

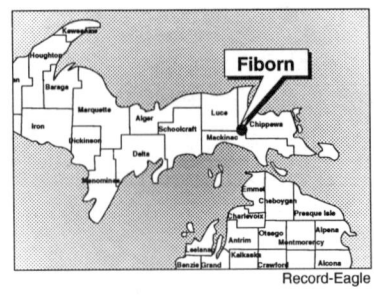
Record-Eagle

In 1904, two unlikely partners teamed up on a project to turn limestone into gold. They were Chase Osborn, publisher of the weekly *Soo News* (and later, governor of Michigan), and William Fitch, president of the Duluth South Shore and Atlantic Railroad. That year they opened a quarry in Mackinac County and began shipping crushed limestone rock to Sault Ste. Marie, thirty-seven railroad miles away. They named the project—and the village they built for the workers—Fiborn Quarry, Fiborn being an acronym or composite of their last names.

The limestone at Fiborn Quarry was an exceptionally pure type of calcite, especially valuable in the manufacture of acetylene gas. Fiborn's biggest customer was a calcium carbide plant at the Soo, which paid them a very good price for the real thing, uncontaminated by iron or other impurities. The rock was shipped over a three-mile spur from the quarry to the DSS & A main line at what came to be known as Fiborn Junction.

The village consisted almost entirely of the quarry workers and their families, who lived in company houses. But it also had a general store and a two-story boarding house that served three meals a day—workers walked there from the quarry for their big noonday meal. The village was granted a post office in 1907, and Samuel B. Martin, general manager of the quarry operations, was its first postmaster.

Among the many interesting things about Fiborn Quarry were its caves. The Fiborn limestone outcrop

A section of the quarry as it looks today.

One of the ruined buildings in the quarry.

is a part of the Niagaran Reef, extending from Niagara Falls to Minnesota, and it was full of caves. They were well known to the earliest settlers, who used them to store perishable food like milk and butter. The practice was taken up by the residents of Fiborn Quarry, too— until the company (which earlier had expressed a desire to preserve them) got greedy, extended its operations into the cave area and almost obliterated them.

Like Tom Sawyer and Becky Thatcher, the village kids were especially attracted to the caves. Despite warnings from their parents to keep away from them for fear of injury or worse, they couldn't resist the temptation to explore them with flashlights, and insofar as the records go, without mishap. The caves contained many passages, some with head room for walking, others with only crawling space. A stream ran through them at the lowest level.

There was a school for the children and during the summer they had no trouble finding other things to do. The quarry operations provided a daily show—big steam shovels loading rock into railroad cars, which in turn went topside and unloaded into the crusher—other trains taking on sized rock from the crusher—dynamite crews drilling into the rock and laying their charges, which sometimes by mistake showered house roofs with rock fragments.

There was good fishing and hunting too, in the big woods all around. Taken altogether, Fiborn Quarry was a pretty good place to grow up in.

But it lasted only about thirty years. In 1909, it was sold to Algoma Steel, which used great quantities of limestone in its blast furnaces before closing down the quarry in the 1920s. It had a brief revival in the 1930s, when its limestone was used exclusively to resurface

The old engine house in the quarry.

US-2—the old highway had been built of an inferior grade of limestone and in a steady rain, turned white and slippery as spilt milk.

The village lost its post office in 1936, and was almost completely deserted by 1940. In 1987, a Michigan forest conservation group known as the Karst Conservancy bought the original Fitch and Osborn holdings. Since then, it has done a good job of managing its 600 acres of quarry and surrounding forest, preserving the wilderness character of the place and protecting its wildlife, while at the same time making like-minded visitors welcome.

The Conservancy includes a spooky kind of forest at its northwest end. Cancer in trees is not uncommon, but in this particular forest is seems to have exploded. Huge malignant growths have formed on what seems to be one out of every two or three trees. Some trees have as many as half a dozen of the unsightly bulges on their trunks. Moreover, it's a dark and damp kind of place, unnaturally silent and menacing almost as if it resented intruders—and no birds sing.

But don't let that deter you. For nature lovers Fiborn Quarry is an otherwise very friendly and hospitable place.

47
Harrietta: Still a Good Place to Live

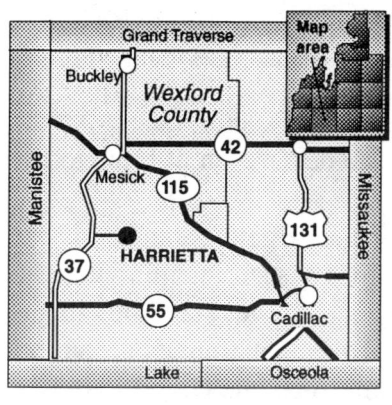

Harrietta was named for a railroad builder and his wife. In 1888, ex-governor of Montana James Ashley, and his two sons, James, Jr. and Harry, had pushed their Ann Arbor Railroad to a tiny crossroads settlement in Wexford County's Boon Township. Here they paused for awhile, bought a tract of land and platted it for a village, which they named Harrietta, a combination of Harry and his wife's name, Henrietta. They built a station and began hauling logs and pas-

The buildings on Main Street are all in good shape, but they've been empty for years. The one at left is the old Brastrom hardware and general store; it was built in 1924.

sengers to Cadillac and points south. Later, the railroad reached its ultimate destination at Frankfort in 1892.

The Ashleys were big, energetic men. Because of their high-handed methods of securing railroad right-of-way for little or nothing—or not even bothering to ask—they had acquired the reputation of buccaneers. At Cadillac, for example, after the Grand Rapids & Indiana Railroad had refused them permission to cross their tracks, they threw a "diamond" across the tracks one night, thus obtaining a right-of-way by usage, and continued on their merry way.

In 1890, a man named Frank D. Gaston platted another addition to the the village and built a sawmill on Slagle Creek. The village was incorporated in 1891 and renamed Gaston. This made the Ashleys very angry. They delivered an ultimatum: either restore the original name of the village or the trains would not be stopping there any more. Horror-struck, the village elders, who knew very well which side their bread was buttered on, hastened to comply. But it would take two years and a special act of the Michigan legislature to get the name changed back to Harrietta.

Meanwhile, the villages had grown accustomed to the luxury of being able to take the train to Cadillac for a day's shopping and entertainment, and then ride it back home at night. You had to be careful, though, not to miss the evening train and get stuck in Cadillac for the night. Cadillac in those days wasn't a nice place to get stuck in, particularly after dark.

Lumbering in the area had already begun under Manistee lumbermen Charles Ruggles and Louis Sands.

The Harrietta Town Hall was a CCC building moved to Harrietta.

and the village began to grow and prosper. In 1893, Frank Gaston and S. P. Millard built a brick factory, and the Fellers brothers built a sawmill and a stave mill in 1897. Other manufacturing establishments included a stove factory and a chemical plant for the manufacture of alcohol and other wood by-products. In 1901, the State built a large fish hatchery on Slagle Creek, and it is still in operation, though on a much reduced scale.

It also had more than 600 inhabitants.

Like most sawmill towns, Harrietta began to decline when the lumbering days came to an end. The decline was slow at first, then quite rapid. What put the final nail in the coffin was the rerouting of state highway M-37 in the 1950s. Until then, Harrietta's location on the old State Road made it a busy place. But the new highway bypassed the village three miles to the west, and left it isolated in a backwash.

Now only the post office, two churches, a community hall, and a few dozen people are left. Some of the old commercial buildings still stand, but they've been empty for years—there isn't a single business in operation. The trains still go by, hauling sand from Yuma, but they don't stop at the village any more.

Harrietta people say that isn't all bad.

Thomas Gray must have had such a place as Harrietta in mind when he wrote *Elegy Written in a Country Courtyard*. It lies in a quiet, green valley with a fine trout stream running clear over a sand and pebble bottom. There are giant shade trees and a small park with swings and slides for the kids. Seniors (and many of the villagers are senior citizens) meet Monday, Wednesday, and Friday for lunch at the town hall. Everybody is related to almost everybody else. Most are ethnic Slovenes whose forebears came from a territory in Yugoslavia when it was part of the Austrian Empire. They bear such names as Lazar, Scerbak, Spolyar, Bayma, Lipar, and Cussins.

Like their forebears they enjoy visiting Traverse City and Cadillac for shopping and entertainment. The only difference is that now they drive automobiles instead of riding the train.

"Traverse City is a great place to visit," says Dan Boehle, who lives in Harrietta but works in Cadillac.

Harrietta's St. Edward Catholic Church was originally St. Ambrose Church in Jennings. It was dismantled and moved to Harrietta around 1920.

"We go to Traverse City almost every Saturday and eat dinner."

"But I wouldn't want to live there," he adds. "Harrietta is a great place to live."

Most Harrietta people feel that way.